The Freedom Trail

Following one of the hardest
wartime escape routes
across the central Pyrenees
into Northern Spain

by Scott Goodall

The Freedom Trail

Published by Inchmere Design
First edition, published in Great Britain, 2005

ISBN 0-9549910-0-1

Printed in Great Britain by Buckingham Colour

Front cover picture: The Col de Craberous (2382m)

Acknowledgements

Dozens of people have helped me with the birth of this guidebook. First on the scene was my very good friend the late Gordon MacDonald, followed by many other wartime veterans from Britain, France, Holland and America, including John Franklin, Fred Greenwell and Sam "Dick" Timmers Verhoeven, whose stories are told in the following pages.

But the completion of this project would never have been possible without the knowledge, help and sound practical experience of all my mountaineering friends in the village of Seix. Colonel Guy Séris and the members of our "Chemin de la Liberté Association" have helped me enormously but a very special "THANK YOU" must go to Monsieur Paul Broué, the late André Desclaux, the late Noel Faur, Monsieur Alain Ferracin and Monsieur Gaby Antras, all "montagnards extraordinaires" who way back in the year 1994, quite literally...showed me the way!

My grateful thanks also to Mark and Alastair Goodall, Alec Willcox and Malcolm Molyneux, whose art, design and production skills are second to none! I am also indebted to photographer Craig Allen, whose excellent pictures appear throughout these pages. Craig can be contacted professionally by e-mail at allenphoto98@yahoo.co.uk

Last but certainly not least I owe a vote of everlasting thanks to my wife Judy whose patience (to borrow the words of Sir Winston Churchill) "is deemed to be considerable", but has been considerably strained over the years by accompanying me during many hours of note-taking, rock-scrambling and swearing at high altitude. Bravo et merci mille fois!

Our local "Chemin de la Liberté" or Freedom Trail Association is now part of an international World War Two Escape Lines Memorial Society, the founder and driving force behind which is the irrepressible Roger Stanton from Harrogate in Yorkshire, a dogged ex-soldier with whom I have hiked many a harrowing mile. Full details of this society (ELMS) can be found on the website: www.escapelines.com Another very interesting and detailed site concerning all aspects of the French "département" of Ariège is: www.ariege.com

During the second week of July every year, an official four-day hike along the Freedom Trail takes place to commemorate all those guides, couriers and safe-house keepers who kept this route open during the last war and in many cases sacrificed their own lives while doing so.

Any individual or military group wishing to take part in this annual event should get in touch with the author...

Scott Goodall *"L'Escrabiche", 09420 Lescure, France e-mail: scttgdll2@wanadoo.fr*

The Freedom Trail

Contents

Introduction **1**

Mountain Safety **7**

Information **9**

    Le Couserans   *9*

    Getting there   *9*

    Local accommodation   *10*

Day One: Saint-Girons to Aunac **13**

    Map: Saint-Girons to Esquenac   *16*

    Map: Esquenac to Aunac   *22*

    History: Murder at the Col de l'Artigue   *26*

Day Two: Aunac to La Cabane de Subera **29**

    Map: Aunac to La Cabane de Subera   *30*

    History: Sowing the Teeth of the Dragon   *33*

    History: Avis/Notice   *39*

Day Three: La Cabane de Subera to Le Refuge des Estagnous . . **41**

    Map: La Cabane de Subera to Le Refuge des Estagnous   *42*

    History: Escape to a Spanish Jail   *48*

    History: Deaf, Dumb and Blind!   *52*

Day Four: Refuge des Estagnous to Alos d'Isil **59**

    Map: Le Refuge des Estagnous to Alos d'Isil   *60*

    History: Once is too Often   *66*

Day Five: Alos d'Isil to Esterri d'Aneu, Spain **71**

    Map: Alos d'Isil to Esterri d'Aneu   *72*

    History: Ambush!   *74*

Appendix **85**

    Le Chemin de la Liberté Suggested Equipment List   *85*

    Space for notes   *86*

Monsieur François Avril,
war veteran and standard-bearer
from the village of Soueix Rogalle

Introduction

et's face it, apart from a few grey-haired crag-rats like myself, the Second World War means very little to our modern generation of happy hikers. Dimly remembered pages in a school history book perhaps, or 'The Guns of Navarone' belching flame and smoke for the umpteenth time on television. All something from Grandpa's era, a succession of noble deeds embedded in a savage past, annual ceremonial events to be remembered and paraded on certain specific dates such as the 8th of May, the 15th of September and the 11th of November.

But to walk 'Le Chemin de la Liberté, or 'The Freedom Trail', from beginning to end is to bring part of that school history book to life and to experience in a very personal way at least some of the dangers and hardships faced by those men and women who used this high mountain escape route during the last war.

More than sixty years have passed since those far-off days, and sixty years is a helluva long time. To understand how and why 'Le Chemin' came into being, it is important to know certain historical facts, so for those who came in late, the scenario went something like this...

In the late summer of 1939, a small but particularly nasty German Nazi by the name of Adolf Hitler, set out to conquer Europe. Like all megalomaniacs, Hitler was not only bold and ruthless, but also extremely efficient. In less than a year, his armies had over-run and occupied Poland, Norway, Denmark, Belgium, The Netherlands and France. By June 1940, the German swastika was flying on every flagpole from the Pyrenees to the Arctic Circle, and from the English Channel eastwards to the Russian border.

Introduction

After the invasion of Great Britain (which was expected to take place in a matter of weeks), and a later invasion of Russia which the German generals were already plotting in secret, Hitler intended to draw up what he called a 'New Order' for the ruling and governing of his vast, Nazi-dominated empire.

The blueprint was diabolically simple. All Jews and the Slavic races of eastern Europe were considered by the Fuhrer to be the 'Untermenschen', or sub-humans, and therefore had no right to live. They would be exterminated. Other conquered peoples such as the Dutch, Belgians, French (and eventually the British), would be employed as slave labour for the benefit of the German master race, shipped out and put to work in factories, mines and farms.

In France however, during the early days of occupation, the Germans decided at first to try a velvet-glove approach to their forced labour plans. Using the Vichy French collaborators and public officials as front-men, they began by asking for young, able-bodied volunteers to leave home and work in the German-run factories of eastern Europe. "La Relève" (which means literally a changing or taking over from someone or something), was a deal in which one prisoner of war would be set free in exchange for every hale and hearty volunteer workman who travelled east. Official, long-term contracts were offered, plus good food, wages and accommodation.

Although the vast majority of Frenchmen refused point-blank, a few did rise to the German bait, tempted no doubt, by the prospect of earning enough to feed their starving wives, children and families back home. But soon the real truth about working conditions began to filter back.

Although all mail between Germany and France was heavily censored, one unemployed tradesman from Toulouse who travelled east to work in a Berlin factory made a special arrangement with his wife. "If," he said, "you receive a letter from me written in black ink, you can believe every word I say. If, however, I write the letter in red ink, you will know I'm lying, and that everything is exactly the opposite of what I have said."

A few weeks later, the man's wife received a letter written in black ink. Her husband, it seemed, was fit, well and happy. In glowing details, he told his wife how pleased he was to be in Germany. The food was excellent, the pay was good, his overseers were kind, considerate and helpful, the work stimulating and not too hard. He had plenty of time off for leisure and shopping. "Here in Berlin," he added as a footnote, "one can buy everything one needs... except red ink."

But in February 1943, off came the velvet glove and down came the iron fist. Infuriated by the near total failure of their volunteer scheme, the Nazi authorities introduced their infamous S.T.O. (Service du Travail Obligatoire), decree. In other words, the deportation to German labour camps of all able-bodied males over the age of twenty.

Two million prisoners of war were already toiling for the Third Reich and the S.T.O. decree added millions more. Husbands were separated from their wives and children from their parents, all rounded up by force and shipped out in railway wagons, usually with very little food or water and certainly no sanitary facilities.

Conditions in the labour camps were appalling. Food was desperately short, winter clothing non-existent, the hours of work long and hard. Doctors and other medical staff and supplies were rarely - if ever - made available, and as a consequence disease was rife. It was against this background of hate, misery and despair that 'Le Chemin de la Liberté' came into being.

All over France, thousands of young men were thinking only of escape. Britain had still not been invaded and was carrying on the fight alone. Although her army had been crushed and humiliated, France still retained the will and the courage to resist her hated German masters. Le tricolore continued to fly with the Free French Forces in North Africa, and in London General Charles de Gaulle was doing all in his power to urge his fellow countrymen to join him in a new fight for freedom.

The direction for the vast majority of would-be escapees was south to neutral Spain. Once across the Pyrenees, there was the possibility of easy access to London or North Africa via British-held Gibraltar. Ever since the fall of France, a network of escape lines had been springing up all over Europe. These were designed not only to help escaping civilians, but also the ever-increasing number of Allied airmen being shot down during missions over Nazi-occupied Europe.

Several of these major lines were in operation throughout the war (the Comète Line, the Pat O'Leary Line and the Marie-Clare Line to name but three), and in each case the procedure was the same. Evading aircrew were passed from link to link in the chain by a succession of local 'helpers', who clothed, fed and hid them, usually at great personal risk to themselves.

Having reached the mountains, the men were then hidden in secret collecting areas and formed into groups ready for the final night ascent to the Spanish frontier. Official statistics tell us that during the wartime years and along the entire length of the Pyrenean chain, there were 33,000 successful escapes by Frenchmen alone. Of these, 3,000 never returned home. Approximately 6,000 Allied servicemen (mainly aircrew), also made successful escapes.

Although the main evasion routes used by the Pat O'Leary line was centred on the Mediterranean coast at Marseille, and the Comète Line concentrated on the Atlantic coast near Bayonne, many other evaders were filtered down through central France to Agen and Toulouse, then on to the central Pyrenees and the starting point of 'Le Chemin de la Liberté' in the small town of Saint-Girons. Naturally enough, as the war progressed, many other escape trails sprang up in this part of the Ariège, each one known only to its particular guide or passeur. Neighbouring towns and villages like Foix, Tarascon, Aulus-les-Bains, Massat, Castillon, Seix and Seintein, all had a network of invisible mountain routes leading upwards to the Spanish frontier. Of the 33,000 French évadés during the war, 782 of them escaped over the mountains of the Ariège, the high point being in June 1943, when there were 113 successful evasions.

But at the beginning of 1943, due to increased German surveillance and often betrayal by Frenchmen who worked for the feared and hated

Vichy-run paramilitary force known as La Milice, ambushes along many of these trails became more and more common. In all, more than a hundred passeurs were arrested and deported or shot out of hand as they tried to flee across the mountain slopes.

But even during the years of high surveillance, our Saint-Girons - Esterri escape route via the soaring massif of Mont Valier, stayed operational and remained so until the end of the war.

It was re-opened and inaugurated in 1994 as an official way-marked hike with a difficulty rating of Grade Three (British equivalent, Grade Five). As well as giving precise details of the trail itself, I have included in this guidebook, a few tales and recollections as told to me by those mountain men and ex-Allied airmen who all - a very long time ago - did it for real!

Bonne chance, bon courage, et bon voyage!

Scott Goodall,
Saint-Girons,
Ariège, France

Bonjour !

Je suis un chien « Montagne des Pyrénées » dit « Patou », je veille sur la sécurité des troupeaux. Mon rôle est de repousser toute présence étrangère aux bêtes que je protège. (Merci de garder votre chien à vos côtés)

6

Mountain Safety

I t must be emphasised that this is not an easy trek. It is an extremely hard and difficult traverse of a high mountain range. The heights to be climbed are up to 2600 metres (8580 feet), not once but twice in a single day (day three). There are snowfields to be crossed and some sections of enormous granite boulders to be negotiated. No particular climbing techniques are necessary but it is a long, very hard upwards slog. Unless you are an accomplished mountaineer, the only feasible months to tackle this route are between the beginning of July and the end of September, when most of the snow will have gone from the high peaks...and before it starts snowing again! Personally, I'd choose late August, early September.

Necessary French maps are IGN (Institut Géographique National) No. 2047OT-TOP 25 ST-GIRONS Couserans; 2048OT-TOP 25-AULUS-LES-BAINS Mont Valier, and IGN Carte de Randonnées...PYRENEES CARTE No. 6 1: 50 000...COUSERANS Valier-Maubermé.

Any well-equipped and prepared mountain walker who is skilled in the use of map and compass (and now the GPS system), should have no difficulty in following the instructions and almost step-by-step details contained in the following guide. The two "TOP-25" maps mentioned above, incidentally, (St-Girons-Couserans and Aulus-les-Bains-Mont Valier), are both GPS compatible.

But please remember...the weather can change very quickly in this part of the French Pyrenees. A morning of glorious sunshine and stunning views can change virtually in half an hour into an afternoon of storms, thick mist and nil visibility. It's really important to remember this and be well equipped for any eventuality. **An appendix of recommended kit to be carried on this four or five-day hike can be found on page 85.**

7

One final piece of advice. In the words of the "Kop" fans of the famous Liverpool Football Club (of which I am not a fan myself but admire from a great distance)..."**Never walk alone**". Go hiking into these mountains with a friend or friends. Always have back-up in case of emergencies. A mobile 'phone is extremely useful these days but it doesn't always work in certain high altitude nooks and crannies. And if you have any doubts whatsoever about the traverse, please contact the Saint-Girons tourist office which will be only too pleased to provide information about professional guides who can accompany you especially on the hardest days three and four of this route - from the Cabane de Subera via le Refuge des Estagnous and subsequently across the frontier into Spain.

It is also prudent to tell the local police (**"La Gendarmerie"**) exactly when you plan to tackle the route, your starting date and proposed finishing date. In this case it is advisable to tell La Gendarmerie in Saint-Girons and more importantly in the village of **Castillon**, near Saint-Girons, which provides the high mountain rescue squad in case of serious trouble. The local tourist office will help you with this as well.

You must also have adequate **insurance cover** to pay for the considerable cost of a helicopter evacuation if this is required. But...hopefully not! **Bon voyage!**

YES
I need help

NO
I do not need help

Signals to helicopters

Information

Le Couserans

Saint-Girons (pop. 6000), is a quiet and attractive town straddling the confluence of three mountain rivers - the Salat, Lez and Baup. It also stands at the entrance to the eighteen valleys of Le Couserans, the former Roman name for this proud and fiercely- independent western part of the Ariege. In the 5th Century AD, the lower valley of the River Salat was a robust and prosperous Gallo-Roman settlement with its headquarters in the neighbouring town of Saint-Lizier, two miles north-west of Saint-Girons on the D 117. Once the ancient capital of Couserans, Saint-Lizier boasts a magnificent Bishops' Palace, museum, and a cathedral in which a rare 18th Century pharmacy has been preserved with great care and pride. A visit to all four of these historical gems is thoroughly recommended.

In July 2005, a "Chemin de la Liberté" or Freedom Trail museum will be opened in the former railway station at Saint-Girons. The museum will in fact commemorate not only our local wartime route but the many others which existed across the entire Pyrenean mountain chain during the years 1940-44.

Getting there

Saint-Girons lies 100 kilometres (60 miles), south and slightly west of Toulouse. In addition to a daily coach service between the two, there is also a rail/coach link. One catches a train from Toulouse (Matabiau station), to Boussens on the Tarbes line, which then connects with a railway (SNCF) 'bus to complete the journey to Saint-Girons.

There is also an international airport at Toulouse Blagnac with at least four flights a day between London Gatwick and Heathrow. Time in the air between Britain and France is one and a half hours.

Local accommodation

A fast finger-count gives a total of six hotels in Saint-Girons varying from Michelin one-star standard to one or two star logis and below. Four camp-cum-caravan sites are situated within a two-mile radius of the town.

These are...

The Parc de Palétès on the D 3 south of Saint-Girons towards the village of Lacourt. It boasts a swimming pool, tennis courts, rentable chalets and a restaurant.

The Parc d'Audinac on the D 627 to the north of the town also has a swimming pool and refreshment facilities.

Two smaller camping a la ferme sites are to be found in the village of **Sentenac** on the D 618 towards Castillon, and at **le Pont de Nert** two kilometres beyond Parc de Palétès at the junctions of the D 3 and D 33 (direction Riverenert).

Full details of these and other nearby sites, plus a list of hotels, Logis de France, B&B and self-catering establishments, are all available from the Saint-Girons Tourist Office. Tel: 05.61.96.26.60. Fax: 05.61.96.26.69. E-mail: otcouserans@wanadoo.fr

Saint-Girons, Ariège

Day One

SAINT-GIRONS (391m, 1290ft)
to AUNAC (766m, 2528ft)

Distance: 23 kilometres (14.37 miles)
Walking time: 8 hours. With rests, allow 9 hours for this stage

Not so long ago, a large and very imposing iron bridge spanned the River Salat on what is now the boulevard périphérique or ring road around Saint-Girons. This boulevard and bridge were once part of a busy railway line linking many towns and villages of the Ariège with their neighbours in the departement of the Haute-Garonne and the major city of Toulouse.

During the wartime years it was southwards from Toulouse and westwards from Foix, that many would-be évadés travelled to Saint-Girons by train. The entire approach to the Spanish frontier had been declared a zone interdite or forbidden zone by the Germans, and those without authorised travel permits were often forced to jump from the train as it slowed down on the outskirts of Saint-Girons and seek what cover they could find in the surrounding countryside. Sometimes a sympathetic train driver would give two blasts on his steam whistle as a signal to jump at a suitable place, and many former evaders have reason to be grateful for the courage of those French railwaymen or cheminots who were also prepared to risk their lives and offer what help they could to the ever-increasing stream of escapees from all over metropolitan France.

In 1991, the proud old Pont de Fer or iron bridge was demolished for safety reasons and a modern concrete span built in its place. On the 8th of May 1995, this new bridge was inaugurated and renamed "Pont le Chemin de la Liberté" and now serves as the symbolic starting-point of this long and arduous mountain trail.

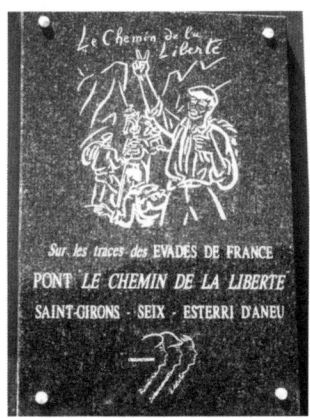

From the engraved marble plaque Pont le Chemin de la Liberté, situated at the western end of the bridge, walk for 200 metres (compass bearing 280 degrees), to a roundabout and turn left into the Avenue de la Resistance, (D.618 signposted for Eycheil, Massat and Aulus les Bains). 100 metres ahead on the left is a Total Garage and Service Station, directly opposite which are two access roads leading to a local housing development known as Beauregard.

Pont le Chemin de la Liberté marble plaque - *a symbolic starting point for the mountain trail*

Take the road on your left and climb a hill to the entrance of La Clairière restaurant (120 metres). Bear sharply right and follow the road to a local 'village hall' known as the Maison de Beauregard (another 170 metres). Bear left past the maison, then immediately right past a street sign saying Allée de Sourroque, over the first junction and into the Rue du Crabère, a sign for which can be seen set into the hedge of a house on the left of the street. 150 metres further on, there is a second sign saying Rue du Crabère which faces you directly ahead. Turn LEFT at this sign into a level grassy track with houses on your left. Continue for 300 metres until you see a green waymark directing you sharply right up a narrower path (often overgrown in summer), between trees and high banks on a compass bearing of 180 degrees. Fields on your left overlook the outskirts of Saint-Girons and the approach to Eycheil on the D. 618.

The path climbs for a few minutes and then enters a wood (usually very muddy at this point), and after a sharp left-hand bend climbs again fairly gently for ten minutes until another green waymark directs you RIGHT once again (compass bearing 270 degrees), on to a secondary track leading up and into clumps of acrid-smelling box trees (buxus sempervirens). Some people like the smell of box trees - I don't! To me it's reminiscent of an army of tomcats on a nocturnal territorial marking mission. After a five-minute climb, the path dips gently downwards, where more green waymarks guide us to the LEFT this time, on to a track once again leading upwards through more box trees. NOTE: On this particular section of the Freedom Trail, several yellow wooden arrows can also be seen nailed to the trees at different points. These refer to various local circuits close to Saint-Girons and should be ignored. The only relevant waymarks for the long-distance "freedom walker", are the occasional blobs of florescent green paint leading him or her ever southwards and (we hope), ever upwards.

Approximately forty five minutes from the start at Beauregard, the beech wood thins and levels out at the top of the hill. Your height now is 660 metres, 2178 feet. Follow the path straight on and down for a few hundred metres, IGNORING a well-cut path on your right (another local circuit) and a yellow cross nailed to a tree on your left, then take the first right-hand grassy path on your right several metres further on. You'll find a green waymark at this fork which leads up to a tarred road. Turn right on reaching the road, and you are in the hamlet of Ouerdes (pronounced Werrrrd), which at first glance appears to be inhabited only by a horde of barking dogs. A veritable melange of size, age, colour, shape and more than a few dubious breeds. All of them though, would appear to be more interested in announcing the presence of a passing hiker rather than biting a chunk out of his leg. Besides, a law in France states that any man-hungry dog (un chien mechant), must be kept firmly under control, ie: tied up or kept behind a secure fence anywhere near a public right of way. If a dog bites, the person bitten has a perfect right to claim insurance or sue for recompense. And that includes doctor's fees against any subsequent injuries or - perish the thought - hospitalisation!

Walk on to the end of the hamlet and the end of the tarred road (ignoring another well-cleared path to the right marked as "Circuit de Parrat") and you'll be faced with a decidedly ugly concrete-block-built tin-roofed garage. A grassy path dips down to the LEFT of this garage and you follow it for approximately five minutes, splashing through a pleasant stream of water, until the path splits and you turn RIGHT and climb steeply for a few minutes up to another tarred road at a farm called Roc de Gabach. A green waymark turns you left on this road and after a short descent - seventy metres or so -you'll find yourself turning sharp

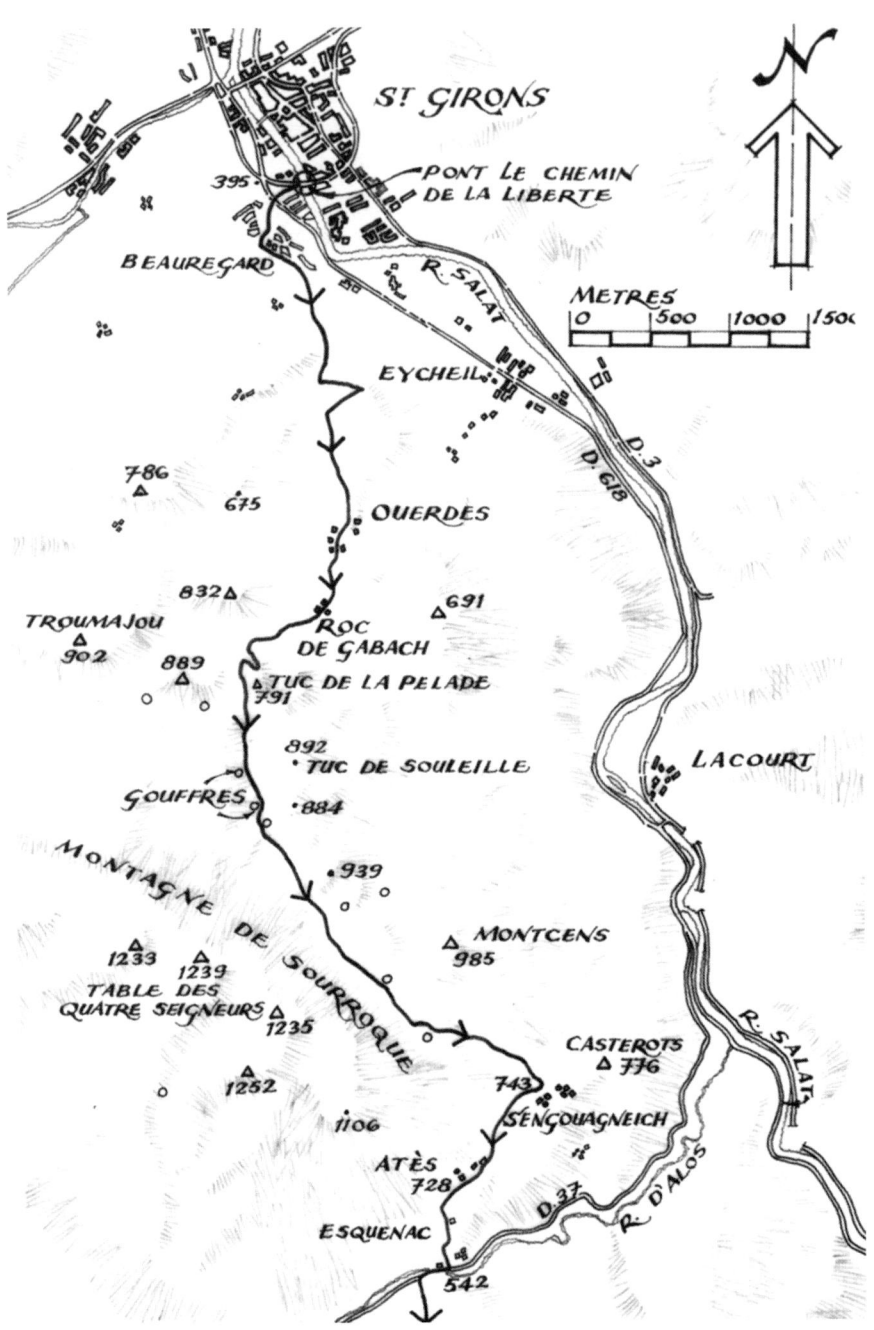

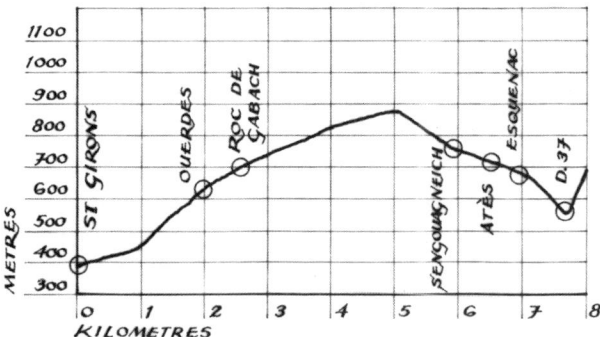

right on to a wide, well-beaten foresters' track signposted boldly as "Route Forestière de Sourroque and "Forêt Communale d'Eycheil". Walk straight on past a sagging hunters' hut on your right and then onwards and upwards through several hairpin bends, passing a sign which says "Table de 4 Seigneurs" and "Lacourt" until you reach a wide open space and a parking area. Keep straight on at this point following signs for "Table de 4 Seigneurs" and "Lacourt", passing another sign "Forêt Communale d'Eycheil". Directly ahead of you now is the soaring complex of "Les Falaises de Sourroque", an impressive vertical cliff towering over a forested landscape pierced and riddled by more than four hundred gouffres or underground grottoes. The department of the Ariège as a whole is renowned for its caves and grottoes, many of them, such as Les Grottes des Niaux, Lombrives, Mas d'Azil and Bedeilhac, being highly regarded by experts all over the world and famous not only for their breathtaking size, but also for the superb quality of their primitive cave paintings and other relics left by the hand of prehistoric man. All of these, including a spectacular boat trip along the underground river network at Labouiche, near Foix, are open to the public during the summer season.

Another kilometre of easy walking will take you to a forestry picnic area. Several marble tables and benches are provided here for your comfort. Bloody chilly to sit on, especially if wet, but you'd probably like a rest by now anyway, so wipe off and enjoy! Approximate hiking time from Saint-Girons to this point is two hours. Height now: 820 metres, 2706 feet.

At the picnic area, turn left down a muddy path when you see a bottle and hamper sign and you'll pass two more signs which announce boldly: "Forêt Communale d'Eycheil, and "Forêt Communale de Lacourt", then the path climbs for a few hundred metres up out of the beech wood to an open space at the top. Your height now is 867 metres, 2861 feet. Bear right at the top, and fifty metres further on, turn LEFT down a path signposted for Lacourt and Segouganeich (local Circuit No. 6).. A thirty-metre descent leads to a gully and a stream. Cross the stream and then turn RIGHT when the path splits. Do NOT follow the Circuit 6 sign leading to your left, but follow the green waymarks up right on to a wide stretch of hillside which is covered with chest-high ferns during the summer and dead (or burnt) bracken later in the year.

Once across this stretch, the well-beaten but bramble-strewn path enters another cool and pleasant beech wood. Gigantic rocks lie scattered to right and left, silent and long-standing monuments to the forces of nature that a very long time ago must have torn them loose from the towering cliffs of Sourroque above and to your right. At a height of 884 metres, 2917 feet, the path starts to descend towards the valley of La Rivière d'Alos. Once clear of the wood, panoramic views open up directly ahead. To the south-west lies the high, rounded bulk of the Cap de Bouirex, and beyond, the even higher, flat-topped massif of Mont Valier (2838 metres, 9635 feet), whose south-east face must be traversed before the Spanish frontier is reached.

An easy, half-hour descent takes you to a minor road which runs through the hamlet of Sengouagneich (impossible to pronounce!). Turn right when you reach the road (green waymark on road) and continue past a strange, dome-shaped building on your left which at first glance appears to be some kind of nuclear fall-out shelter but which in actual fact is a local chateau d'eau or water reservoir. A further half-kilometre stroll will take you to the hamlet of Atès (pronounced At-ezzz), and yet another dubious horde of barking dogs. Here again, the same rule applies. Ignore them all and march on! The decibel level might be high but the danger level is low! Walking time from Saint-Girons to Atès: two hours, forty minutes.

As you enter the hamlet, there is a thick hedge on your left. Look for a green waymark on the road almost directly opposite the first farmyard on your right. A grassy path (a local commune "sentier"), leads you left off the road down for fifty metres before turning sharply right and continuing to descend towards the valley, river and minor road (D.37), now seen clearly below. The villages of La Rivière and Alos are directly in front of and below you.

The path leads straight down past several barns and thirty minutes' easy descent (following several green waymarks) will take you to the rushing stream of "La Rivière d'Alos" which flows through the valley sheltering the tiny ancient village of La Rivière itself. A bridge crosses the river and you reach the minor road D.37 having descended to a height of 542 metres (1788 feet).

Now - as always - you have to start climbing again! That's the name of the game! Turn right uphill (there's a green waymark on the road) and two hundred metres past the "La Rivière" village sign, you'll see another couple of green waymarks directing you up an unmarked road on your left. This climbs steeply to the picturesque village of Alos, where during the war many evaders were led at night by local passeur Etienne Andreu past the shuttered houses and into the darkness of the hills beyond.

It's a steep 15-minutes climb to the village, where on your left as you enter it you'll see a quaint "lavoir" and a cool, refreshing fountain. An excellent place to re-fill your water bottles.

Turn left past the Mairie on to the D 37 road to Seix and follow it for 50 metres round a bend until the road forks. Take the narrower road which rises steeply on your right, and past a large signpost marked for "Col de la Plantach", "Chemin de la Tire" and "Pic de la Quere". Pass a house with green shutters on your left and then go straight on very steeply up a narrow path between high banks. You'll see a green waymark on a stone in the middle of this path.

15 minutes' hard upwards slog from Alos you'll come to a minor road. Cross it and take a path bearing left into a beech wood. After 50 metres

bear right and climb steeply again, this time following the regular yellow and white waymarks which will guide you through this silent, impressive forest, known locally as the Bois de Plantach.

Another 30 minutes will take you to the summit and the Col de Plantach at 997 metres (3290 feet). From the two barns at the top, pause for a few minutes and gaze to the south. On a clear day the view is breathtaking, and the lace-like scars of the numerous pistes or ski slopes at the Guzet-Neige winter sports' complex can be clearly seen.

We're about to lose height now. The path dips downwards following a signposted track for the Col de l'Artigue, and an easy fifteen minutes' descent will take you to the Col itself at a height of 880 metres (2904 feet). Turn right along a track bordering a chicken wire fence (ignoring another track signposted for the Col de Catchagnede), and 50 metres further on, turn left down a wide grassy path signposted for Escots (30 minutes). There is a green waymark at this point too.

But...before you descend, look up at the slope which dominates the right-hand side of the main track (compass bearing 280 degrees). Two hundred metres above you, in a grove of trees, is a small barn in which nineteen year-old mountain guide and passeur Louis Barreau was trapped and subsequently killed by the Germans in September 1943. **(See "Murder at the Col de l'Artigue", page 26)**

A small marble cross has been erected at the spot. The epitaph says "En Memoire de Louis Barreau. Mort Pour La France. Le 12-9-43. A l'Age de 19 Ans". He was later buried in his family tomb in the village of Sentenac d'Oust which lies in the valley five kilometres below.

You're losing height again now but the descent from the Col de l'Artigue is an easy walk down a wide grassy track. You'll pass two picturesque stone barns on your right and soon after pass through a small wooden gate. Keep walking straight on at this point. In the valley below, slightly west of south and on a compass bearing of 190 degrees, you'll see the village of Sentenac d'Oust and the conifer-covered, almost artifical-looking 'tit' of a mountain known as Le Bois de Cos.

The hamlet of Aunac and (presumably), the end of your day's march, lies slightly to the west and at the base of this peak.

The track now descends fairly steeply, past a high wire fence bordering a large private house and then joins another track which is part of a local "GR Pays" circuit. There is a wooden signpost here, so turn right following the sign for ESCOTS (5 mins), drop down through another wooden gate and on to a wide gravel "road". This section of the trail is way-marked quite clearly from now on with yellow and red signs on appropriate trees!

Five minutes' walk down the gravel road you'll see a house on your left and a signpost on your right which announces that you have now reached the Col d'Escots at a height of 725 metres (2392 feet).

There are also direction arrows pointing you towards "Gite d'Aunac" and "La Souleille des Lannes (15 mins)" March straight on past a house on your right until the path splits again. Then take the right-hand fork, straight and level, through another wooden gate, and then - please - pause and look at the view!

On a clear day, there are awesome views of the mountains on your right. The flat, chopped-off summit of Mont Valier, then the Pic de Pomebrunet, the Pic de Lampau, and to the extreme right of the massif, the deep, narrow 'V'-like cleft that marks the Col de Craberous at 2382 metres, 7860 feet. If you're going to succeed and escape into Spain, this is the Col that must be crossed in two days' time. It ain't easy, so... bon courage, mes amis!

On again, through yet another wooden gate and down past a small château d'eau or water reservoir until the path splits again. Simply follow the wooden direction arrow for "Souleille des Lannes (5 mins)" and sure enough - in five minutes - you'll find yourself passing a fairly derelict and firmly shuttered restaurant called "L'Auberge du Roy". Directly ahead is the Village des Vacances called La Souleille des Lannes. This is a purpose-built and self-catering holiday village of chalets, studios and apartments which can be rented at reasonable cost during the summer. A swimming pool and children's play facilities are all available.

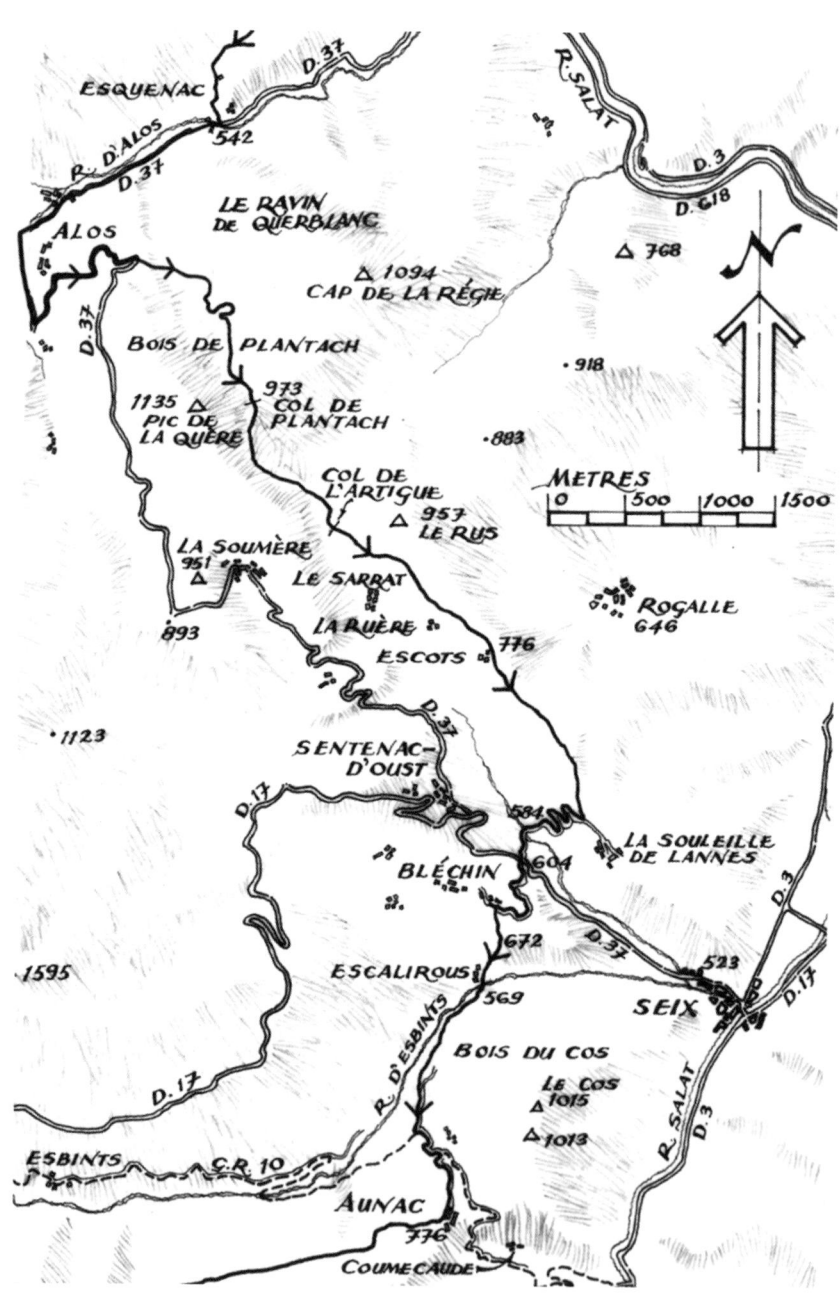

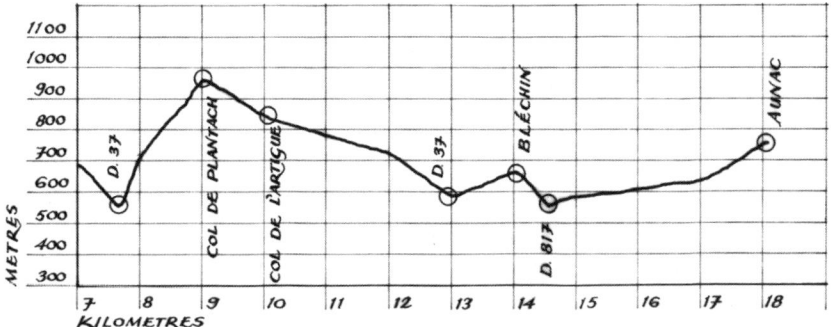

Once past the restaurant on your right, there is a boring fifteen-minute descent of the tarred hairpin approach road to the village which then meets the Seix - Sentenac d'Oust road, the D.37. The picturesque village of Seix is only two kilometres away in the valley below. It bustles with life in both summer and winter, fishing, canoeing, hang-gliding, mountain walking and biking during the warmer months, skiing of all kinds at the nearby resort of Guzet-Neige when the snows come. There is also a varied selection of shops, restaurants and hotels.

Back on The Freedom Trail at the D.37 Seix - Village de Vacances road junction, turn right, and almost immediately opposite, you'll see the D.237 road signposted for Blechin, Bouche, Cerizols and Serre-de-Nougue. Follow this minor road upwards for half a kilometre, and just before the blue and white 'Blechin' sign, turn left up a beaten earth track (green waymark on a tree stump to your left). After 150 metres, take the right-hand fork (another green waymark plus the yellow and red GR Pays sign), then up and down a gentle zig-zag slope towards a three-house (deserted) hamlet known as Escalirous. Just before the hamlet, turn sharp left down the GR Pays path (there are two green waymarks on fence posts at this point), and descend rapidly to a minor tarred road leading to the hamlet of Coumet. Turn left here, down the hill, straight on past another minor road leading to the hamlet of Esbints, and then turn right across a narrow stone bridge which crosses the mountain stream known as le Ruisseau d'Esbints. Just before the bridge there are signposts directing you to "Sentier d'Interprétation du Cos" and "Gite d'Etape d'Aunac"

Immediately after crossing the bridge, turn right (following the "Sentier d'Interprétation du Cos" sign and 50 metres further on, bear left up a narrow enclosed path between overhanging trees - just before an abandoned tennis court. Why anyone would have wanted to build a tennis court at this particular point is completely beyond me! Anyway, on and up...follow the path for about five minutes and you'll reach a minor tarred road leading to the hamlet of Aunac. Cross the road and follow the "Cos" path once again, up into the deep woods. After a right-hand bend the path heads arrow-straight (almost boringly so after a long day's march) for 35 minutes until we reach a collection of converted barns and houses known as Camp de Peyret. Halfway up this stretch there is a path on your left leading to the summit of "Cos" itself. Please ignore this and keep plodding straight on and up.

The Camp de Peyret is at 750 metres (2475 feet). From there, a wooden signpost directs you on towards the Gite d'Etape at Aunac, but before the final walk up to the gite, you will find a marble memorial stone erected in honour of all those escaping Frenchmen (Les Evadés de France), who traversed the Pyrenees only to find that their new-found "freedom" was terminated for several months and even longer by the ever-open jails of General Franco's fascist government. The plaque says simply:

> **"Ils choisirent la périlleuse aventure du passage des Pyrenées pour l'honneur de servir."**

> *They chose the perilous adventure of crossing the Pyrenees for the honour of serving (their country).*

During the wartime years, the isolated hamlet of Aunac was used regularly as a secret collecting area for would-be evaders trying to escape into Spain. Local guide and passeur Isidore Andreu lived here, and it was in these woods and scattered barns that hundreds of desperate people from all over France and other parts of Europe came to seek a final means of escape from the misery and death of Hitler's much-vaunted millenium of Nazism.

Local man Paul Broué, who crossed the border in June 1943 with his friend Antoine Zurlo, remembers those days vividly. "The older people who were trying to escape stood very little chance," he told me sadly. "They were mainly from the north, often city types who had never even seen a mountain before, let alone tried to climb one. They were dressed in city clothes, wore city shoes and were often carrying suitcases filled with what possessions or valuables they had managed to take with them. The Germans had set up a checkpoint on a small bridge in the valley below the track that leads to Aunac. And in those days it was a track, not a tarred road as it is now. With the help of dogs it wasn't too difficult to flush out groups of weary strangers who had no local knowledge, no papers and obviously nowhere to go." Paul also remembers several groups of Jews being rounded up in his area near the village of Seix and their subsequent internment in an hotel in the spa town of Aulus-les-Bains. These Jews, like many others held in the notorious transit camp of Le Vernet, near Pamiers in the eastern Ariège, were subsequently shipped out to various Nazi concentration camps in eastern Europe and never heard of again.

Back to the Freedom Trail! After this long and hard eight hours' march from Saint-Girons, a truly warm welcome awaits you in le Gite d'Etape la Souleille d'Aunac. From the memorial stone, follow the track to the gite upwards for ten minutes through three hairpin bends and then swing left through a dark and mysterious tunnel of box trees to the complex of barns beyond. A cheerful band of barking Pyrenean shepherd dogs will announce your arrival. The gite is perched on a pleasant grassy plateau overlooking the hamlet of Aunac and comprises three converted buildings which can sleep up to thirty people in dormitory-style accommodation. Relax, have a shower and admire the view. Either cater for yourself or order cooked meals from the superb menu provided by Claudine and François...they are "inoubliable"! There are also excellent camping and car parking facilities at the gite.

History of the Freedom Trail
Murder at the Col De L'Artigue

In and around the Ariège villages of Seix and Sentenac d'Oust, the family name of Barrau is not only well known, it is treated with a respect bordering on reverence. In 1943, with the German S.T.O. deportation procedure in full swing and an increasing number of refugees fleeing southwards in an attempt to cross the Pyrenees, Norbert Barrau and his brother Jean selflessly offered their services as mountain guides and passeurs. Their luck ran out in April 1943 when they were arrested, imprisoned and subsequently deported. Both died later in a German labour camp.

It was now the turn of Norbert's sons Louis and Paul Barrau - lads aged nineteen and twenty - to carry on with the dangerous work that their father and uncle had started. Paul remembers those days well. "It was impossible to make daily trips to the frontier, so we had to wait until refugees were collected into groups of up to thirty or more, before a crossing attempt could be made. This meant hiding them and feeding them in isolated mountain huts and barns. The ascent to the frontier was always made at night, and I was terrified of meeting a German patrol. Although I myself knew the mountains well and might have been able to slip away and escape, I knew the refugees wouldn't stand a chance."

During the night of 12th September 1943, young Louis Barrau was waiting alone in an isolated barn above the village of Sentenac d'Oust, on the windswept grass plateau that is the Col de l'Artigue. He was expecting a party of would-be escapees who were being guided up from the valley of the River Salat by a friend of his. Instead, it was a well-armed German patrol that appeared out of the darkness, backed up by local police.

Louis Barrau had been betrayed. It was common enough in those days, especially after the formation of La Milice, a feared (and hated), paramilitary force of thirty thousand French volunteers who worked for the Vichy government and collaborated actively with their Nazi rulers.

Nicknamed Les Souris Grises, or Grey Mice, their task was to hunt down and eliminate any Jews, resistance fighters, communists and Gaullists: in other words, anyone who was directly opposed to the regime of the Third Reich.

Surrounded and trapped in his lonely barn, nineteen year-old Louis Barrau was called upon to surrender. He refused. The Germans then set fire to the barn and Louis made a run for it through the flames and drifting smoke. He was shot down and killed before he had covered fifty metres. Today, a simple marble cross marks the spot where he died close to the route of Le Chemin de la Liberté...The Freedom Trail.

Also hunted by his betrayers and the Germans, Louis' brother Paul was forced to flee. For five days and nights he dodged his pursuers by keeping constantly on the move. Eventually he escaped into Spain and was promptly imprisoned in Lerida jail. "By the time I was released several months later," says Paul, "I had lost ten kilos in weight. My companions and I were handcuffed and moved south to Malaga to await embarkation to North Africa. The final insult came when I was accused of being a spy and subjected to several gruelling interrogations. Once I'd managed to convince the authorities that I was a true patriot, they wanted me to parachute back into France and form a Maquis resistance group. This offer I decided to turn down, so I eventually joined De Gaulle's Free Forces and fought with them until the end of the war."

Paul Barrau, now in his eighties, still lives today in the village where he was born, less than half a mile from the spot where his brother was killed.

Paul Barrau *- hunted for five days and five nights*

Day Two

Aunac: (766 metres, 2527 feet)
to La Cabane de Subera: (1499 metres, 4946 feet)

Distance: 16 kilometres (10 miles)
Walking time: 6 hours. With rests, allow 7 hours for this stage

When the Freedom Trail was re-opened and inaugurated back in 1994, this second day's hike followed the original wartime route from Aunac upwards through a secondary jungle of ferns, brambles, bushes and any other clinging-enveloping-tearing types of undergrowth you care to mention.

For interested map freaks it passed a miniature waterfall called La Fontaine de la Gore (although there's not a drop of blood in sight), then on and up to a height of 1436 metres (4738 feet), at La Mede and Les Champs de l'Ars before emerging at le Col de Soularil.

In recent years, however, due to extensive forestry work in this area, the original route either no longer exists or is totally impassable.

So for Day Two's hike, the scenario now goes like this: Walk back down to the memorial stone from the gite d'etape at Aunac, turn left on the descending tarmac road and after approximately 200 metres (on the first hairpin bend), you'll see a wooden direction post on the left directing you down into the woods on the GR 10. This is one of the well-known "grand randonnée" routes which exist all over France and are well-maintained and easy to follow thanks to their regular red and white waymarks. This section of the route is clearly marked on the French IGN Map (Institut Géographique Nationale) 2048 OT - Top 25 - Aulus-Les-Bains...Mont Valier.

An easy thirty minutes' descent through the beech woods will take you across two wooden bridges into the valley below. After the second bridge, turn right and follow the track until it meets a minor road. Turn left and plod up this road (30 minutes) until you reach the hamlet and

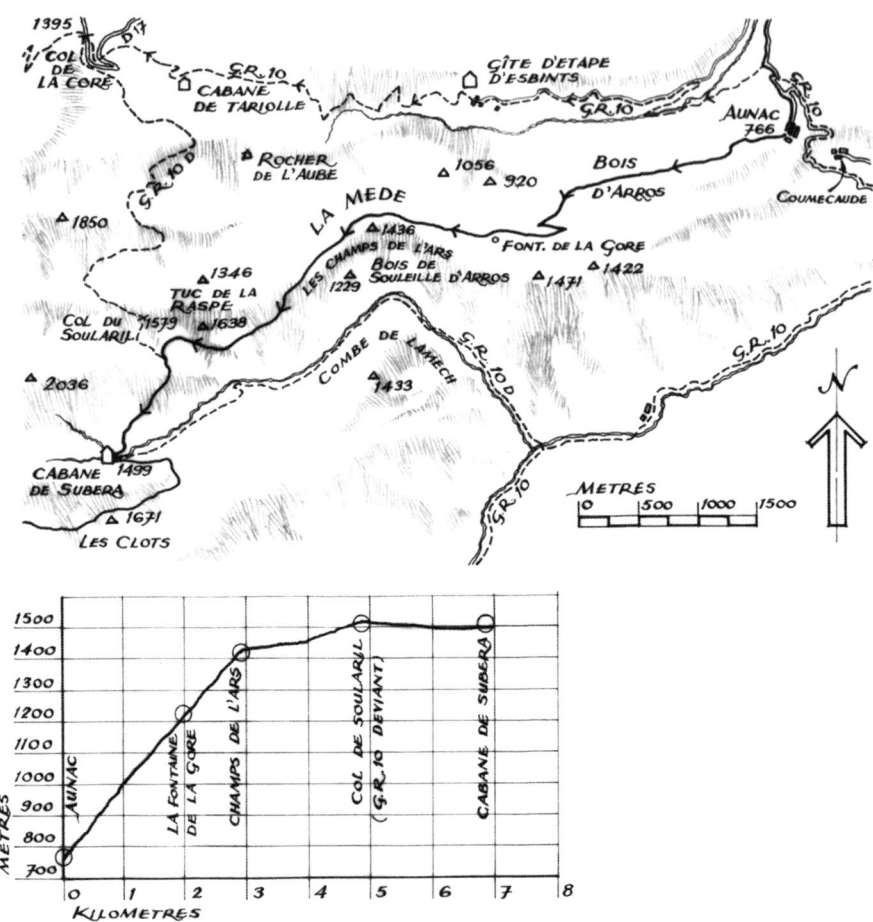

gite d'etape d'Esbints. This is another possibility for accommodation if the gite at Aunac is full during the summer months. Again, as at Aunac, a delightful welcome awaits you!

You're now into the woods again, following a gentle path onwards and upwards towards le Col de La Core. After passing" Les Granges Artigues d'Esbints" (several ruined barns), you'll climb steeply up to La Cabane de Tariole at 1179 metres (3890 feet). This is a hiker's refuge, always open, and can be used in bad weather or the odd emergency!

Another 30 minutes or so, following clear GR 10 red and white waymarks plus wooden direction arrows, you'll arrive at the Col de la Core, 1395 metres (4603 feet). Magnificent views in all directions from here, and yet another monument to the guides or passeurs who led so many people to freedom during the years 1940 to 1944. The memorial honours all those who led the evaders from the local villages of Castillion, Oust and Saint-Girons.

Now descend from the Col de la Core in the direction of Seix, (300 metres or so) and on the first left hairpin bend you'll find an imposing notice board telling you what lies ahead on the final two days of "Le Chemin de la Liberté" or Freedom Trail. The path to la Cabane de Subera is directly up past the notice board and is again a variation of the GR 10 and regularly way-marked with red and white signs. During the war, this was the path used by young Louis Barrau when he led evading Frenchmen and shot-down allied pilots during their approach to the high peaks and their final ascent to the Spanish frontier.

It's a two-hour hike to La Cabane de Subera, passing first of all the unoccupied Cabane de Luzurs (where a murder was committed some years ago when a drug-crazed hippy stabbed his equally drug-crazed girlfriend to death), then on to the quaint Cabane de Casabède, occupied during the summer months by a shepherd and - of course - his vast flock of sheep. Good source of water here if you need to refill your bottles.

Black Merens horses -
a famous Pyrenean mountain breed

On and up now, still following the GR 10 signs to the Col de Soularil at 1579 metres (5210 feet). Excellent views from here, below and to your left the smooth, vertical wall of granite known as "Le Rocher de l'Aube" or Dawn Rock, named, one assumes, for a very obvious reason. From the Col it's downhill all the way (40 minutes or so), to la Cabane de Subera at an altitude of 1499 metres (4946 feet).

The mountain refuge of Subera sits neatly positioned at the head of the Combe de Lamech and is dwarfed by a towering, semi-circular wall of rock known as Le Cirque de Lameza. During the summer months, the refuge is a busy place. La transhumance - the seasonal movement of livestock from the valleys to the high mountain pastures - takes place in mid-June. From then until late September or early October, cattle, sheep and horses graze on the surrounding slopes, looked after by a cheerful shepherd who occupies one half of the cabane during these three to four months. The other half - the hikers' refuge - is open all year round but without a permanent warden. It has double-tier bunks, foam mattresses and can sleep up to twelve people in a certain degree of intimacy. ie: flat out, side-by-side, nobody move, nobody snore, nobody fart, sardine style. There is a sink with piped cold water, a table, benches, several half-

used candles and a fireplace (gather your own wood from the surrounding slopes), for cooking and heating purposes. Toilets? Head for the hills. Usual rules apply. Walk at least two hundred metres before...

La Cabane de Subéra - *1499 metres*

History of the Freedom Trail
"Sowing the Teeth of the Dragon"

They say that all is fair in love and war, but Flight-Sergeant John Franklin certainly wouldn't have agreed with that when less than seven weeks after being married to his sweetheart Beryl, he found himself dangling from a parachute one thousand feet above the blacked-out and misty plains of the Charente region of south-western France. It was 0200 hours on the 6th of April, 1944.

John and Beryl Franklin
on their wedding day

As an aircrew Wireless Operator serving with 644 Squadron R.A.F. based at Tarrant Rushton in Dorset (motto: "We Sow The Teeth Of The Dragon"), John was part of a six-man Halifax bomber crew that had taken off late the previous evening on a "special operations flight" over enemy-occupied Europe.

The Halifax was a heavy bomber powered originally by four 1145 h.p. Rolls-Royce Merlin X engines. At the outbreak of war the 'plane hadn't even made its maiden flight, but by the end of November 1940 it was in full service with R.A.F. Bomber Command. As the war progressed the aircraft's power was increased to four 1615 h.p. Bristol Hercules XVI radial engines with a range of well over one thousand miles.

Apart from its bombing role, the Halifax was used for carrying paratroops and as a gilder-tug on such memorable missions as 'Operation Market Garden' (The Battle of Arnhem), and the June 1944 D-Day landings in Normandy. Another very important role for this aircraft was to fly lone, unescorted sorties over enemy territory at low level in order to drop arms, ammunition and explosives to various resistance groups operating throughout occupied Europe.

John Franklin and his comrades were taking part in just such a mission when they ran into serious trouble in the wee small hours of 6th April, 1944. Their destination was to the south of the Charente region and at first all went well. There was a clear, moonlit sky which allowed for good navigation and no German night-fighters were encountered on the low-level crossing of the French coast. The Halifax was flying at two thousand feet and a dropping zone for the arms and explosives was to be marked out by flashing lights from the ground. These in fact never appeared, and after circling the area several times, pilot Flight-Lieutenant Frank Cleaver had no option but to turn and head for home with the Halifax's cargo of weapons and supplies still intact.

The aircraft's new course towards the Atlantic coast took it within range of German anti-aircraft batteries protecting an airfield on the outskirts of Cognac. For the British airmen it became not only brandy country but bandit country as a vast ring of heavy guns opened up. Overhead at less than two thousand feet, the Halifax was a proverbial sitting (or flying) duck. Hit by a barrage of fire, the starboard wing caught fire and unable to maintain height, pilot Cleaver gave his crew the order to bale out.

John Franklin exited through the bottom hatch and, after a few heart-stopping moments as he yanked at a reluctant ripcord, his 'chute opened and he landed safely in a field. Soon after burying his parachute, he found Flight Engineer Ray Hindle, dazed by his low-level jump but also unhurt. The blazing Halifax had disappeared from view and there was no sign of the rest of the crew. It seemed to John and Ray that they were the only survivors, but Navigator Norman Wyatt and Bomb Aimer Alan Matthews had also managed to bale out successfully. Matthews landed in the River Charente and was rescued by a local Maquis group. Wyatt was captured soon after and spent the rest of the war as a prisoner. The pilot, Flight-Lieutenant Cleaver, stayed at the controls of his blazing bomber, crash-landed in a field and escaped seconds before the 'plane blew up. For his outstanding skill and courage that night, Cleaver was later awarded the Distinguished Flying Cross. Out of the six-man crew there was only one fatal casualty. Rear Gunner Donald Hoddinott died when his parachute failed to open properly.

Like so many other downed Allied airmen before and after them, John and Ray knew that a successful escape and a safe return to England depended on two things: help from the local population...and a helluva lot of luck! For a French civilian to be caught aiding a shot-down airman meant death or deportation **(see page 39)**, but despite the appalling risks there was always someone, somewhere, who was willing to take those risks.

The luck that Franklin and Hindle so desperately needed seemed to be holding when the following day they approached a local farmer and were able to swap their R.A.F. uniforms for civilian clothes, but the two men ran into trouble soon after when they knocked at the door of a lady's house clutching the yellow "translation cards" that were part of every airman's survival kit. They asked for food by using the word "affamé", which means famished or starving. If this word is mispronounced it can easily sound like "femme" or woman, and John and Ray found the door slammed firmly in their faces by an indignant French housewife who obviously thought that the two scruffy-looking individuals on her doorstep were after something far more titillating than a hunk of bread and cheese!

But the real breakthrough in the men's fortunes came on the 9th of April. Eight miles south of Perigueux in the departement of the Dordogne, they reached the village of Marsaniex and were directed to the house of the parish priest. He was in contact with a local Maquis resistance group whose members were also working for an Allied escape network codenamed the Pat O'Leary Line which specialised in funnelling civillans and servicemen south to the Pyrenees and subsequently into Spain.

After a careful and detailed identity check to make sure that they were not German spies, John and Ray were issued with false papers and smuggled southwards to Toulouse by a variety of means and a variety of girl couriers who were risking their lives daily to keep the men free and on the move. It was now the end of April and Franklin and Hindle had been on the run for more than three weeks, but it was in the city of Toulouse that the men were at last able to rest for a few hours and prepare themselves both physically and mentally for the mountain challenge that lay ahead.

Formed in May 1940 to help thousands of British servicemen still stranded in France after the evacuation of the main Expeditionary Force from the beaches of Dunkirk, the Pat O'Leary escape line was originally centred on Marseille and the Mediterranean coast, but in 1943 the network was penetrated by a French traitor known as Roger le Legionnaire who was working for the Gestapo. As a result, dozens of 'helpers' and 'safe houses' were betrayed and many of the line's leading members arrested, tortured and deported. Several were to die later in German concentration camps. One prominent figure in the Pat O'Leary organisation, however, did manage to escape detection. Her name was Marie-Louise Dissard (codename Françoise), surely one of the most doughty, pugnacious and resourceful women ever to have served with the French Resistance. Ex-school teacher and First World War nurse, sixty three year-old Francoise was running a dressmaking business in Toulouse when Hitler and his stormtroopers began to goose-step all over her beloved France in May 1940.

Her hatred for the Nazi and Vichy French regimes soon boiled up into a constant and all-consuming passion. By December 1942 she was a vital link in the Pat O'Leary network and it was she who took control of the shattered remnants of the line when it was betrayed in 1943. Françoise trusted no one except her pet cat Mifouf, was thought by her immediate neighbours and the local Gestapo agents to be slightly mad, and it was probably a combination of the two that saved her from arrest when the Nazis pounced.

Monument to "Françoise" Dissard in Toulouse

Her apartment in the Rue Paul-Meriel in Toulouse became one of the most important safe houses in the south of France, a final rest and recuperation centre before the dangerous sixty-mile journey to la zone interdite, the forbidden frontier zone and the various towns and villages in the département of the Ariège such as Foix, Tarascon, Saint-Girons, Seix, Oust and Sentein, where weary groups of evaders would be hidden and fed before setting off with their guides along the Freedom Trails and across the snow-capped Pyrenean peaks to sanctuary in Spain.

Safe (albeit temporarily), in Dissard's Toulouse apartment, John Franklin and Ray Hindle rested and slept soundly until they were literally shaken awake on the night of 1st/2nd May 1944, by an R.A.F. attack on a local aircraft factory which was led by Leonard Cheshire's 617 Pathfinder Squadron and backed up by a force of Lancaster bombers from 5 Group. John Franklin remembers the incident well. "I heard the sound of Mosquitoes across the rooftops, flying low. At that time I believed the railway system was the target, because of the chaos at the main station next morning when Ray and I left for the Pyrenees accompanied by a courier."

But the night raid proved to be a blessing in disguise. With the station itself unserviceable, lorries were laid on to ferry passengers to and from the train which was waiting down the line and therefore well away from the usual military checkpoints. The journey south took less than three hours. When the train stopped it was at a small station in the foothills of the Pyrenees. John Franklin is still not sure of the exact location but thinks it could well have been Saint-Girons.

The courier then directed his charges towards a battered old 'bus waiting in the station yard. The windows were broken and boarded up and all the seats had been removed. Other evaders then began to appear mysteriously from various directions and soon a large group had formed. There was one other R.A.F. man ("George",who had been hidden for three months in a Paris brothel prior to his escape bid); the rest were downed American fliers. As the 'bus moved off, the men were ordered to lie flat and face-down on the floor until they had reached the small town of Saint-Gaudens, approximately forty kilometres to the west of Saint-Girons. There, a Basque guide was waiting to lead them up into the mountains on the last and most difficult part of their long walk to freedom. For most of the men it was a gruelling, exhausting climb. They were not only badly-clothed and shod and suffering from the lack of a proper diet, but weeks of danger, enforced concealment and generally living on their nerves, had also taken their toll.

On day two they reached a remote mountain hut where the guide left them, saying that he'd return early the next morning. For some unexplained reason he did not return and when a German patrol was spotted in the valley below, John, Ray and an American named John Betolatti, decided to split from the main group and strike out for the border on their own.

By dusk on the 4th of May 1944, they were working their way along the side of a precipitous gorge five hundred feet above the River Garonne as it foamed and gushed along on its endless journey between Spain and France. The men knew they were getting close to the border but the question was, how close? Without the expertise of their guide there was no exact way of knowing when they had crossed that invisible line between imprisonment and freedom.

John Franklin again: "We were edging our way cautiously along in the darkness when we were suddenly faced with a vertical slope at the top of which we could make out a tall, square shape which we thought could well be an enemy pillbox. We monkeyed our way towards it and found to our delight (and relief) that it was a giant billboard saying VIVA FRANCO...ESPANA, in big bold letters. We'd made our escape! We were on Spanish soil!"

The three men had actually crossed the frontier high above Le Pont du Roi, or King's Bridge, which spans the River Garonne at this point. Deciding to play it safe, they kept out of sight until they had reached the town of Vielha, another twenty six kilometres to the south. There they were arrested by the Guardia Civil and handed over to their respective Consuls.

On the 6th of June 1944, John Franklin and Ray Hindle found themselves taking off from Gibraltar in an R.A.F. Dakota bound for England...and home. It was exactly two months to the day since they had baled out of their burning Halifax bomber over Chateauneuf-sur-Charente in enemy-occupied France.

Avis

Toute personne du sexe masculin qui aiderait, directment ou indirectment, les équipages d'avions énemis désçendus en parachute, ou ayant fait un attérrissage forcé, favoriserait leur fuite, les cacherait ou leur viendrait en aide de quelque façon que ce soit sera fusillée sur le champ.

Les femmes qui se rendraient coupables du meme délit seront envoyées dans des camps de concentration situés en Allemagne.

Les personnes qui s'empareront d'équipages constraints a attérrir à leur capture, recevront une prime pouvant aller jusqu'à 10,000 francs. Dans certains cas particuliers, cette recompense sera encore augmentée.

**Paris, 22 septembre 1941.
Le Militarbefehlshaber en France,
Signe: von STULPNAGEL.
Génèral d'Infanterie.**

Notice

Any male person directly or indirectly helping the crews of enemy aircraft landed by parachute, or having effected a forced landing, or assisting in their evasion, or hiding or helping them in any way whatsoever, will be shot immediately.

Women guilty of the same offence will be deported to concentration camps in Germany.

Any persons apprehending crew members having effected a forced landing or descended by parachute, or who, by their attitude, contribute to their capture, will receive a reward of up to 10,000 francs. In some cases, this reward will be higher.

*Paris, 22 September 1941.
The Military Governor in France,
Signed: von STULPNAGEL.
Infantry General.*

A suitcase radio - used by Special Operations Executive agents during the war. They were extremely heavy!

The wreckage of Halifax Bomber MZ 981, 644 Squadron RAF

Day Three

La Cabane de Subera (1499m, 4947ft)
to Le Refuge des Estagnous (2245m, 7408ft)

Distance: 13 kilometres (8.12 miles).
Climbing time at a medium pace: 7 hours 20 minutes. But with
(very necessary) rests, it is advisable to allow 9 or 10 hours for this stage.

From the front door of the cabane, head east-south-east (compass bearing 110 degrees), for approximately 450 metres to reach a narrow gully and a two-strand barbed-wire fence. Climb over (or crawl under) the wire for a five-minute walk through a beech wood and across a slope of loose scree. Shortly after crossing a mini-waterfall and stream, the 'Chemin' bears RIGHT off the main path and begins to climb. Blobs of yellow paint mark the way, but look carefully, because they're not too easy to spot.

A ten-minute stiffish ascent leads you to another two-strand barbed-wire fence. Beyond lie open mountain pastures, the only sounds on a clear, still day being the distant tinkling of cow bells and the plaintive 'pee-weeeee' of a circling buzzard. Local wildlife is rich and varied. As well as the buzzards, vultures, kites and eagles soar above the highest peaks. Take care at this point and look for the rather evasive yellow waymarks.

The 'Chemin' rises steeply now, leading us past 'Les Clots', the local name for a series of shallow depressions in the turf reminiscent of English dewponds. Height: 1671m (5514ft). Clumps of wild azaleas cover the ground and huge clods of mountain turf have been dislodged - overturned and uprooted as if by the hands and spade of a demented gardener seeking a plot of fertile soil. These manic diggings are the work of les sangliers, or wild boar, pushing and prodding with their stunted snouts in search of worms and succulent roots. Nocturnal by nature, these animals usually lie half-buried and hidden in muddy wallows or "bauges" during the hours of daylight. Butterflies abound and grasshoppers leap for safety at

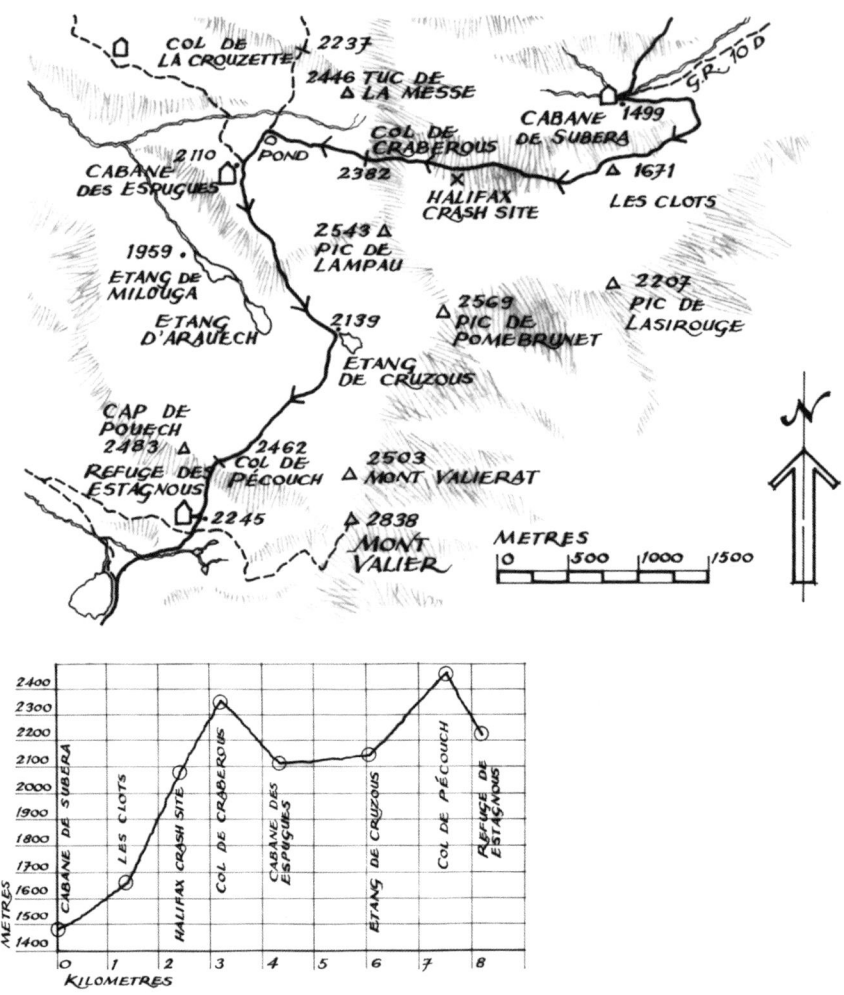

every step, legs propelling them upwards, forwards or sideways with all the grace and agility of miniature trampoline artists.

Mountain ponies of the Merens breed also roam these upper slopes. Sturdy and sure-footed, jet-black in colour, they are highly respected for their strength and endurance and were used, it is said, as pack-horses during Napoleon Bonaparte's ill-fated march on Moscow in 1812.

1 Annual Freedom Trail ceremony, on the bridge at St-Girons

2 An early start. Into the Pyrenean foothills

3 The monument to passeur Louis Barrau, at the Col de l'Artigue (see page 26)

4 Heading south, towards the village of Alos

1 **Getting steeper** ...lower slopes of Mont Valier

2 **Mountain guide, mountain cool!**

3 **Local shepherd** from the valley of Esbints

4 **On the Col de Craberous** (2382m)

5 **Reaching the snowline** near the
Col de Pécouch

6 **Blizzard!** Refuge des Estagnous,
14th July 2002

Looking up and south towards the Pic de Lampau

1 *Sunset over the Pic de Barlongère*
from the Refuge des Estagnous

2 *A hint of bad weather to come*
on Day Four

3 *Lac Long* (2125m)

4 *One kilometre from freedom* ...but the Col de Clauère must be climbed first!

5 *Last snowfield below the frontier*

6 *The Spanish border* ...looking back down at Lac Long

1 Due south, *a panoramic succession of high peaks*

2 The final descent, *towards the river Noguera Pallaresa*

3 Safety in Spain! *End of the trail*

Ahead, the Pic de Lampau prods at the sky like a giant molar. It's at this point, an hour and a half from Subera that you might trip over a half-hidden black plastic pipe apparently coming from nowhere out of a slab of rock on your left and plunging downwards over a sheer cliff to your right. This pipe carries the water supply to the cabin more than 200 metres below. Who performed the Herculean task of laying the pipe, when and how, remains a mystery that is unlikely to be solved

Wreckage

It's at a height of 2200m (7260ft), and two hours' climb from Subera, that the first pieces of wreckage are to be found, small and gleaming in the sun. They fill you with surprise at first and then - as they get bigger - a sense of sadness. Jagged, almost sculpted chunks of aluminium lying scattered over the mountainside. Here a rusting oxygen bottle, there a tangle of metal, a section of fuselage and part of a twisted wing, topped by a simple metal cross.

Sixty years ago, on the 19th of July 1945, a four-engined British Halifax bomber from 644 Squadron based at Tarrant Rushton in Dorset, took off on a cross-country training flight to the south of France. It carried a crew of seven, all young men in their twenties.

The intended route was south to Toulouse, then east to Sete on the Mediterranean coast. The return flight would have taken the aircraft westwards to the Atlantic, then home via the Bay of Biscay and the extreme western tip of Brittany. Instead, for some inexplicable reason, the Halifax swung south and west and crashed into the Pic de Lampau in the heart of the Pyrenees and more than eighty kilometres off its intended course.

Flight-Sergeant Donald Thorne, Halifax pilot - and stone plaque in memory of the seven dead crew members

43

The cause of the accident was put down to navigational error and a strong, mistral-type wind that was blowing at the time. All seven members of the crew died on impact and a memorial stone bearing their names now marks the spot where their lives ended so tragically.

Directly ahead is a steep climb to the Col de Craberous at 2382m (7860ft). There are two possibilities now. From the wreckage of the aircraft and the memorial plaque, either head due west (compass bearing 270 degrees), up and into a steep-sided and very impressive gully of giant granite rocks and loose scree, or follow the green direction arrows pointing up a steep grass slope to the right of the Halifax wreckage on a compass bearing of 320 degrees. This second option skirts the Craberous gully and guides you to the top section on a slightly easier - but still pretty hard climb.

Until mid-July, the greater part of the Craberous gully is full of firm, packed snow (un néve), which can make for easier going provided care is taken. A stout walking pole or ice-axe and lightweight crampons are advisable for this section.

We're in marmot country now, so keep your eyes peeled for this thickset, ground-dwelling relative of our friendly squirrel. Marmots have coarse-furred coats of yellowish brown, are between 30 and 60 centimetres in length, can weigh up to 7 kilograms, have strong feet and claws well adapted for digging, and live in burrows high on the mountain slopes. They're often seen sitting bolt upright on boulders keeping watch over their immediate territory. When alarmed (and often just for fun), they emit a shrill, high-pitched whistling call uncomfortably reminiscent of someone's dying scream. The sound is so sudden and unexpected that it can easily scare the goretex pants off any unwary walker!

The upper half of the valley is extremely steep and you can expect to take an hour and twenty minutes from the crash site to the saddle of the Col de Craberous itself. Here, another plaque has been placed in memory of all those men who have passed this way before - not for the pleasure of walking but for the honour of serving that greater cause called freedom..

Magnificent views bombard the senses. To the east, an ever-descending panorama of hills, ridges and mist-smothered valleys. To the north lies the Col de la Crouzette, south, the menacing summit of Mont Valier at 2838m (9365ft), is an ever-present challenge and straddles the border between France and Spain.

East face of Mont Valier
- from La Cabane des Espugues

The descent from the Col de Craberous to the second mountain refuge 'La Cabane des Espugues', can only be described as dizzy. Three hundred metres straight down and no messing! A hectic, foot-scrabbling slide that can easily start a landslide of loose rocks and scree, so watch out for any companions below. As on the approach to the Col, this descent is also partially snowbound until mid-July, so the usual precautions must be taken.

Again, yellow blobs of paint mark this fifty-minute, straight-down descent which leads to grassy moorland and a circular dried-up étang or pond where a clearly-defined path swings left and leads you directly to the Cabane des Espugues less than one kilometre away.

La Cabane des Espugues

At 2110m (6963ft), the cabin of Espugues is open all the year round, but without a warden, or non gardée. Again, it can sleep twelve people in our intimate sardine style: three tiers of bunks and mattresses, plus a fireplace and a two-ring stove fed from a bottle of butane gas. Also some candles...and a small wall cupboard in which I can personally testify to finding an unopened bottle of wine obviously left by some previous (overburdened? careless? forgetful? newly-teetotal?) hiker of unknown nationality. Anyway, cheers mate! A votre santé! As for fresh water, a mountain spring can be found bubbling into a stone reservoir on the slope just below the cabin.

Thirty metres in front of the refuge is a dark and gloomy grotto. 'Espugues' is the Greek word for grotto, hence - naturally enough - the name of the cabin. An attempt has been made to fence off the entrance and inside it is extremely dark and extremely cold. A strong sense of preservation prevents one from exploring any further, deeper or lower! In any case, the grotto is filled with snow and impassable until mid-July.

Directly ahead is the rounded mass of Mont Valier, the upper slopes also blanketed in hard-packed snow until late July. From the cabin door, head south-east on a compass bearing of 140 degrees, climb the first small hill and then pick up a well-beaten path winding its irregular way towards the head of the valley. Below and to your right, two small mountain lakes, the Etang de Milouga and the Etang d'Arauech, reflect perfect images of the sky and the jagged rocks above. Here too, herds of fleet-footed izards can be seen leaping from crag to crag. In the massif of Mont Valier at least, this Pyrenean cousin of the Alpine chamois is protected by law and safe from the hunter's gun.

The path is easy to follow now, with blobs of blue paint and strategically-placed stone cairns leading you onwards towards a third lake, the Etang de Cruzous. Thirty minutes after leaving the cabin of Espugues, the path gives way to jumbled granite blocks that form the lower slopes of Mont Valier's north-east face. Here, green waymarks and more small cairns guide you ever upwards for approximately fifty minutes. The route then swings right parallel to the summit, again marked by green stripes and stone cairns. Another fifty-minute traverse will guide you to a saw-toothed gap in the mountain ridge known as the Col de Pécouch (2494m, 8230ft).

Before the end of July this traverse will be across hard-packed but fast-melting snow, while in late summer, water-smoothed rock slabs interspersed with deep gullies of huge boulders will have to be negotiated. From the Col de Pécouch, the refuge des Estagnous can be seen 250 metres below, lying snuggled at the base of Valier's granite crest. A steep, straight-down descent of forty minutes (again through possible snow patches), will take you to the refuge. Approximate time from Espugues to Estagnous is 2 hours 50 minutes.

Le Réfuge des Estagnous, used regularly during the wartime years by various mountain guides and the exhausted men whom they were trying to smuggle to freedom, can now accommodate more than sixty people in the cheerful togetherness of its high-altitude bunk-bed system! This, most surely, is the Hilton, Savoy and Ritz of all the local refuges! There are two dining-rooms, toilets, showers and washbasins, even electric light supplied by a generator. Friendly wardens are in situ from mid-June until the end of September and excellent four-course evening meals are provided. Home-made vegetable soup, pasta or rice with succulent casseroles (even breast of duck on occasions), and cheese followed by gateaux. Wine is also on sale, plus beers, soft drinks and various aperitifs such as pastis, muscat and vin cuit. Lunches too, are available on request, and breakfast consists of a choice between coffee, hot chocolate and tea, with bread, butter, jam and marmalade. Helicopters normally fly in the necessary supplies but when the weather is bad, mules are used as transport and make an infinitely more satisfying picture for the intrepid Freedom Trail hiker. See here!

A brochure about the refuge and full tariff details are available from the Saint-Girons tourist office.

Mule-train to Mont Valier!

History of the Freedom Trail
Escape to a Spanish Jail

During the wartime years, Jean Souque was a primary school teacher in the village of Seix. Like so many other young men of the Ariège, he had decided to refuse "Le Service du Travail Obligatoire" (the dreaded S.T.O. Order), and avoid deportation to Germany by fleeing across the Pyrenees into Spain.

His close friend Albert Dougnac had already been hiding in a barn at Oust for several months, waiting for suitable escape arrangements to be made, and at midnight on the last day of June 1943, the two men made their way up through the hills to the nearby village of Alos. This was where two of the local 'passeurs' lived, the brothers Jules and Etienne Andreu. In a neighbouring barn, more would-be evaders were gathered and waiting.

At three-thirty in the morning, a column of eighteen men led by Etienne Andreu set out for the Spanish frontier. It was pitch dark and pouring with rain. Not exactly ideal conditions for a stiff mountain climb, but foul weather made the possibility of running into a German patrol far less likely. Nil visibility, sodden bodies and aching limbs were all preferable to recapture, imprisonment or even death.

Each man carried a small rucksack filled with enough food (usually bread, sausage, cheese and a few bars of chocolate), to last for two or three days, but several of the escapees came from far-flung parts of France. They were badly clothed and shod and this was their first contact with the mountains.

Jean Souque's main worry was his friend Albert Dougnac. During the months of hiding and waiting, Dougnac had rarely ventured out during the day, his only exercise being short strolls near the barn after dark. He was certainly in no condition to traverse a mountain chain and became exhausted very quickly. Souque did what he could to help and urged him on.

After a short pause at eight in the morning, the column pressed onwards and upwards through ever-constant rain and lowered clouds. Only Etienne

Andreu knew the invisible way ahead. Twelve hours after that first halt, the mountain refuge of Estagnous loomed out of the mist. Here, in the shadow of Mont Valier and at a height of 2245 metres, the exhausted group spent the night.

At five o'clock next morning, the alarm was raised. Germans were patrolling on the lower slopes and there was no time to lose. In single file, the men made a fast, dangerous descent through thick mist from the Refuge des Estagnous to the shores of the Etang Rond.

For Jean Souque, the 200-metres' ascent from Etang Rond to Etang Long is one he'll never forget. "it was awful," he recalls. "Visibility was nil, one slip meant certain death, and Albert Dougnac was at the end of his tether. I pulled him, I encouraged him, I even carried his rucksack. Somehow we made it."

A snow-filled gully now led to the Col de Clauère, and the column of men reached the top at nine a.m., just as the sun rose above the crest. Here - at last - was the frontier, and the peaks of the Spanish Pyrenees unfolded beyond for as far as the eye could see. Passeur Etienne Andreu now took his leave of them. "Although he asked for nothing, we gave him all the money we had," says Jean Souque. "He headed back down the mountain almost at a run, because too long an absence from home was bound to arouse suspicion. I heard afterwards that Etienne himself had to flee to Spain two months later. Someone had spotted him and reported him."

At six o'clock that evening, the escapees walked into the tiny Catalan village of Alos d'Isil. In theory they should have been safe and celebrating as free men. But the reality of the plight they now found themselves in was quite different. For several years, General Franco's Fascist government had been quietly sympathetic to Adolf Hitler and the German cause. It was a well-known fact, for example, that escapees caught on or near the French/Spanish border were promptly handed back to the Nazi authorities. Although shot-down British and American airmen were usually repatriated swiftly with the aid of their respective consulates, no such help was forthcoming for the thousands of fleeing French and other European civilians.

Day Three

Next day the group was transported by 'bus to the city of Lerida. More interrogations followed. In the hope of obtaining a quick release, Jean Souque tried to pass himself off as a serving French-Canadian military man, but no one believed his story. Within hours he was in prison, confined with several other young men who had crossed the border weeks before. "Some of my friends were there," says Jean, "but I hardly recognised them. Their heads had been shaved, they were thin and very weak, all suffering severely from the effects of dysentry."

Antoine Zurlo, who had crossed the Pyrenees three weeks earlier with his friend Paul Broué, also has vivid memories of the same prison. "Two hundred of us were crammed into one bare room," he says. "The only spaces Paul and I could find to lie down was on either side of a stinking squat toilet. Within days, everyone was infested with lice and fleas. We slept on the floor and were kicked or beaten awake each morning by the surly Spanish guards.

"Mealtimes were a joke. First we had to stand for anything up to two hours in an open courtyard under the blazing sun. The 'food' when it came, consisted of a lump of bread the size of a man's fist and a tin of tepid water in which a few haricot beans could be seen floating. The lid of the tin folded in half served as a spoon. The guards were also under orders to shoot at any man who was seen peering out of the barred window of his cell."

Altogether, eight hundred men were living together under appalling conditions, many of the escaping Frenchmen thrown in with Spanish political prisoners and common thieves. Several were under sentence of death and awaited execution from one day to the next.

As if toying with their captives like those proverbial pawns in a deadly game of chess, the Spanish authorities would liberate small groups of French prisoners from time to time by choosing names at random from a list. Jean Souque tried to impersonate someone else and was found out. Punishment: one week's solitary confinement in the 'mitard', a circular pit twelve metres deep and not quite wide enough at the bottom to lie stretched out.

Release for Antoine Zurlo came at last on August 15th, 1943. Freed by the Red Cross, he spent the next two months in Barcelona before being shipped out with many of his comrades in a convoy of railway cattle trucks. They travelled south via Madrid to Malaga, where General Franco had made certain commercial arrangements with de Gaulle's Free French Forces in North Africa.

It was a barter deal pure and simple - one bag of wheat in exchange for one free Frenchman. Cargo ships full of grain would sail from Casablanca to Malaga. Once unloaded, they would return to North Africa with human cargoes of freed men.

Antoine Zurlo and Jean Souque were just two of those freed men. Having reached Casablanca by the most perilous and tortuous of routes, they enlisted in the Free French Forces of General de Gaulle and fought for their country until the end of the war.

In Jean Souque's own words: *"You never really know what freedom is until you've lost it."*

*After his escape along the Chemin de la Liberté in 1943, **Paul Broué** spent his 20th birthday in Lerida jail and several weeks in the Concentration Camp of Miranda del Ebro before being released to serve with General de Gaulle's Free French Forces in North Africa.*

History of the Freedom Trail
Deaf, Dumb and Blind!

At the end of May, 1943, a tall, well-built young man in his twenties was helped down from a train that had just arrived at the station in Saint-Girons. He was wearing old but respectable civilian clothes, a pair of stout boots and dark glasses. He had travelled by rail from Agen via Toulouse and Foix and his papers stated that he was a deaf, dumb and blind pilgrim bound for the town of Lourdes. The object of his visit was to pray for a "miracle" cure.

The papers were false. Behind those dark glasses lay the nervous but all-seeing eyes of Second-Lieutenant Harry E. Roach jnr., navigator of an American B-17 bomber (the famous Flying Fortress), which had been blasted out of the sky above a German submarine base at Saint-Nazaire on the Atlantic coast less than four weeks before.

Of the bomber's ten-man crew, Roach was the only member still at large. Six of his comrades were dead, the remaining three prisoners-of-war. The daylight raid on Saint-Nazaire had taken place on the 1st of May. Flying at 20,000 feet, seventy eight aircraft from four U.S. Army Air Force Bomber Groups had crossed the English Channel in a series of tight 'V' formations and turned towards the heavily defended German U-Boat base on an east to west approach.

Roach's 'plane was part of the 303rd Bomb Group and was flying that day as 'Tail-End Charlie', the very last aircraft in the vast aerial armada. For daylight raids to be successful the heavy, concentrated firepower of a close-knit bomber formation was a vital means of defence against the swarms of German fighters which constantly buzzed and harried the lumbering B-17s.

Over the target, a barrage of shells lanced skywards as the German 88-millimetre anti-aircraft guns opened up. Plagued by one faulty engine which had been spluttering and shuddering since take-off, Roach's aircraft slowly lost height and dropped back and out of the all-important formation shield.

It was just the kind of damaged straggler that the German fighters had been waiting for. Within seconds they were attacking the solo craft from ahead, above and below. Pilot Jay Sterling tried to regain height by jettisoning his two massive one-ton bombs, but even this sudden lightening of the load could do nothing to relieve the fury of the German attack. Riddled by cannon shells, the radio room and intercom system destroyed, flames bannering back from its number three engine, the B-17 lurched violently to the right and began to nose-dive towards the ground.

Navigator Roach was a big, powerful man, but it took him many agonising seconds to wrench open the emergency exit hatch which was built into the floor on his left. As the metal panel flew off, the aircraft side-slipped into a spin and Roach was thrown head-first into space, closely followed by top turret gunner Sergeant Everett Griffin.

A few moments later the fuel tanks blew up and the bomber disintegrated in mid-air. The results of this violent explosion were two-fold. It undoubtedly saved the lives of co-pilot John Neill and bombardier David Parker, both of whom were trapped in the forward section of the aircraft until the blast blew them clear. For the remaining crew members it was too late. Pilot Jay Sterling was already dead and the others stood no chance as they were enveloped in a swirling mass of flames and debris.

The survivors parachuted to safety and landed well apart from each other in a flat, fertile area divided into dozens of small hamlets and communes. All four men were suffering from shrapnel wounds and turret gunner Griffin had also been badly burnt. He was arrested almost immediately and taken to a German military hospital suffering from severe shock. Co-pilot John Neill was also out of luck. Having injured his neck during the descent he landed badly and broke his left ankle. Although helped initially by several local French farmers, Neill was captured eighteen hours later as he hobbled in agony towards the fishing port of Pornic, a few miles south of the spot where he had landed. Bombardier David Parker had lain hidden in some bushes (minus a flying boot which he'd lost in mid-air), until dawn on May 2nd. Wet, hungry and aching all over, he decided to take a chance and ask for food at a nearby farmhouse. As the owners were ushering him inside, the Germans arrived on a door-to-door search and Parker was arrested and marched off to captivity.

The risks being run by any French civilians who gave aid to downed Allied airmen were amply illustrated during the search for John Neill. Someone had reported the fact that certain locals had shown him a place where he could hide and had given him some bread and wine. Within hours, the commander of the German garrison in the area had ordered hostages to be taken. All the residents of the hamlet and the neighbouring farms were arrested and taken to Nazi headquarters. Brutal interrogations followed, plus a threat to burn down every home unless Neill was handed over immediately. Fortunately for the people involved, the pilot was alone when he was captured that same night in Pornic and the hostages were released without any further charges being brought.

By nightfall on May 2nd, nine of the downed fliers had been accounted for and only navigator Harry E. Roach jnr., remained a free man. Like John Neill he had been helped on day one by several local farmers and had even been given a civilian jacket and a pair of trousers as he headed south and east towards the small town of Chauve. There he was extremely lucky to make contact with a local priest who was a member of the Resistance. The priest's name was Jean-Baptiste Serot and within twenty four hours, Roach had become just one more "parcel" being passed from hand to hand along a major European escape network known as the 'Comete Line'. Set up in the Belgian capital of Brussels in May 1940, this organisation usually channelled its hundreds of fleeing airmen, Jews and other political undesirables south-westwards towards Bayonne and St. Jean de Luz and then into Spain (often by truck), across the extreme western edge of the Pyrenean chain.

But by the Spring of 1943, the Germans had tightened their border controls, sealed off all the major crossing points and increased their surveillance along the entire five hundred-mile length of the French-Spanish border. Circumstances had changed dramatically, as Harry Roach was soon to find out!

On May 4th, the navigator was presented with a bicycle and the address of a safe house in Agen, a town situated in the departement of Lot-et-Garonne and more than 500 kilometres (312 miles), to the south-west. Roach covered the distance in five days, riding along minor roads and country lanes during the day and taking the not inconsiderable risk of asking for food (and sometimes shelter), at night, by knocking on the doors of remote farmhouses. Some of the locals helped him, other were too afraid.

The American's luck held even after his arrival in Agen late in the evening of May 9th. Unable to find the address of his safe house and faced with the prospect of being caught on the streets after curfew, he became desperate and knocked at the door of a villa in the centre of the town. The woman who answered was on friendly terms with the owner of a nearby cafe-cum-dance hall called the 'El Dorado'. The owner's name was Jean Thibaut and he had friends who were working for the Resistance, one of whom was an Irish priest by the name of Patrick Kelly.

So once again it was a man of God who came to the aid of young Harry Roach! But helping the American was not going to be easy. Several of the escape networks (including 'Comete'), had been infiltrated and betrayed and many Resistance workers rounded up and shot. All movements southwards to the Pyrenees had been halted for security reasons.

Roach hid in the Thibauts' house for more than two weeks. It was during this time that the family decided he should learn to play the part of a deaf and dumb man in order to conceal his all-too-obvious lack of French. Pots and pans were dropped behind Roach's back, doors were slammed suddenly and his name would be bellowed out when he was least expecting it. As the days passed, Harry gradually acquired a dull, deadpan expression and perfected the art of total non-response to any violent or unexpected noise.

One night in late May, two men and a woman came to ask Roach a series of questions. They were from the escape line network and they were in no mood to take any chances. Many of their comrades had been tortured and killed and there was every possibility in their minds that the so-called American navigator might be a German spy. If Roach had slipped up on any of his answers, he would have been shot on the spot and his body buried in a nameless grave.

Fortunately for him, he passed the test and left by train for the Pyrenees next morning, his deaf and dumb disguise now extended to that of a blind man also, a helpless pilgrim bound for Lourdes and his hoped-for "miracle" cure.

Waiting to greet Harry as he stepped off the train in Saint-Girons was a local man named Jean Soum. Jean had received his S.T.O. "call-up" that month, but like so many other young men of the Ariege, had taken the decision to escape across the mountains into Spain and find a way of joining General de Gaulle's Free Forces in North Africa.

On the night of June 2nd 1943, the party (which had now grown to forty-plus), set off along Le Chemin de le Liberté led by Jean Soum and a local guide. They scaled the snow-bound Col de Craberous with difficulty and struggled on towards the soaring flank of Mont Valier.

On the second day as they neared the Col de la Pale de Clauère and the Spanish frontier, a lone German fighter, a Messerschmitt, flew low over the tops of the peaks. Roach and his companions dived for cover among the jumbled boulders and it was with an enormous sense of relief that they realised the pilot hadn't spotted them.

By day three they were at the end of the trail in Esterri d'Aneu, but there was no welcome from the surly local police. As usual, everyone was driven south to the regional capital of Lerida, stripped, searched, given a haircut that was more like a scalping, and then thrown unceremoniously into jail. When the American embassy was notified of Roach's escape, it moved swiftly and efficiently as always. Within three weeks, the young navigator was back celebrating with his comrades in England.

Local Saint-Gironnais Jean Soum was less fortunate. He spent six months in a Spanish jail before being released to serve with de Gaulle's Free French Forces. Trained in America as a pilot, Jean returned to Saint-Girons after the war and became a successful businessman. For many years he was a staunch supporter and organiser of European rugby matches between his native town of Saint-Girons and teams from England and Wales, notably Oxford University and Llanelli. Jean Soum died in 1998.

Harry E. Roach died nearly ten years after the war while still serving with the American Air Force, this time as a pilot. He was killed when his jet aircraft crashed on a cross-country flight in 1954.

AIR FORCES
Escape & Evasion Society

Part of a letter of tribute

"The loss of every Allied plane shot down over Europe was a tragedy – every member of a crew that was found and saved and sent back to us brought joy to all his comrades. To everyone who joined in this great work and to each member of his family and to all who shared, in those days, his risks and dangers I send assurances of my deep and lasting gratitude."

Sincerely,

Dwight D Eisenhower

58

Day Four

Refuge des Estagnous (2245m, 7408ft)
to Alos d'Isil or the larger village of Isil (1300m, 4290ft)

Distance: 20 kilometres (12.5 miles).
Climbing and walking time: 7 hours.
With rests it is advisable to allow 8 hours for this stage,
with overnight stop in the village of **Isil***.*

From the front door of the refuge, the 'Chemin' descends steeply in a south-westerly direction (compass bearing 225 degrees), towards the aptly-named Lac Rond lying at 1929m (6365ft). Yellow signs and stone cairns mark the way down on a well-trodden path, at first following the right bank of a stream and then crossing it to hug the towering rock wall and scree slopes which border the lake. Approximately 45 minutes will take you to the water's edge, then turn left - heading southwards on a bearing of 180 degrees - to follow the shoreline on another well-beaten path regularly waymarked with orange and white blobs of paint.

Lac Rond (above) and Lac Long (below) - on the way to the Spanish frontier

A steep climb and a height gain of 200 metres then follows to the (also aptly-named) Lac Long at 2125m (7012ft). The ascent will take approximately 50 minutes and care should be taken when crossing a narrow rock chimney near the top and working your way along a bush-covered cliff-edge with a sheer drop to your left. Fortunately there are now "mains courants" or fixed hand-cables to help you over these most difficult sections.

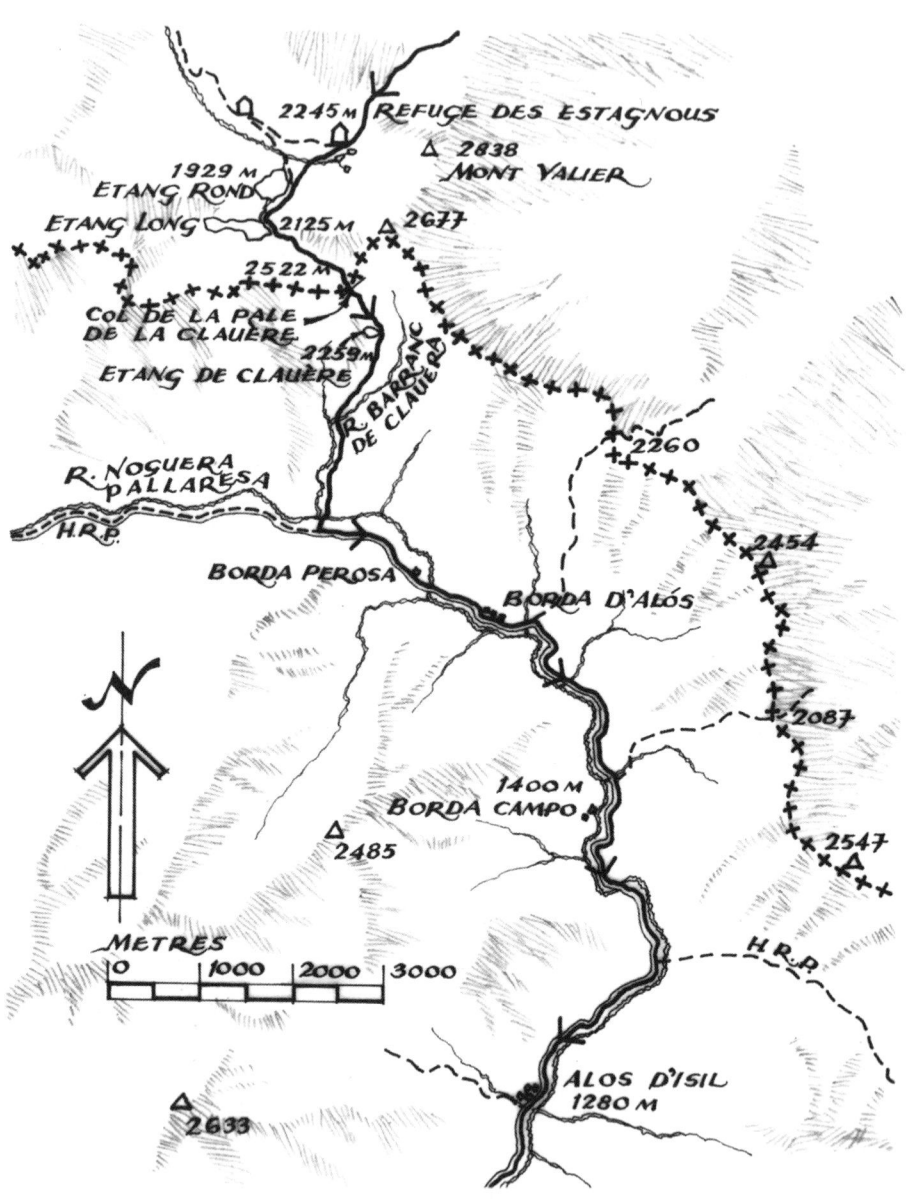

2245M REFUGE DES ESTAGNOUS

△ 2838
MONT VALIER

1929 M
ETANG ROND

ETANG LONG   2125 M   △ 2677

2522 M

COL DE LA PALE
DE LA CLAUÈRE
2159M

ETANG DE CLAUÈRE

R. BARRANC
DE CLAUÈRE

R. NOGUERA
PALLARESA

H.R.P.

2260

BORDA PEROSA

BORDA D'ALÓS

2454

2087

1400 M
BORDA CAMPO

△
2485

2547

N

METRES
0   1000   2000   3000

H.R.P.

△
2633

ALOS D'ISIL
1280 M

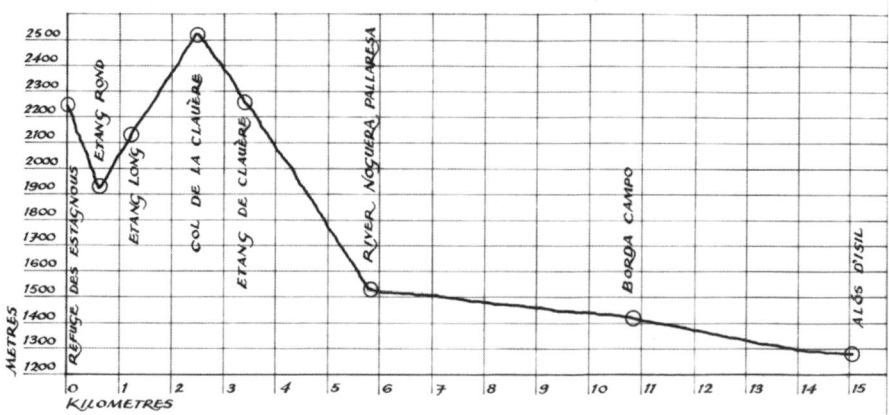

Here on this ledge, pause and reflect for a few moments. Look straight down at certain death and try to imagine what it must have been like for those guides and fugitives of long ago who, in order to avoid any prowling German patrols, were forced to climb this particular section of the escape route during the hours of darkness and often in the snowbound months of April and May, when thick cloud and icy conditions only added to the multitude of dangers. For Jean Souque and his friend Albert Dougnac, the ascent of this cliff and indeed the entire journey in June 1943, was little short of a nightmare.

From Lac Long to the Spanish frontier at the Col de la Pale de Clauère will take approximately one hour twenty minutes. Head south-east on a bearing of 130 degrees, walk up and over the first hillock on a clearly-defined path, then plunge down into a narrow, boulder-filled ravine. Here the path vanishes but small stone cairns mark your way on and up. NOTE: Until mid-July, deep, hard-packed snow covers even this lower section and the entire approach to the Col ahead.

The ravine climbs steeply and widens out into an extremely steep-sided valley filled with loose scree and more firmly-packed snow. The presence of this permanent néve makes for easy climbing, a firm upwards plod that will take you steadily higher towards the sharp outline of the crest directly above. Many izards roam these valley sides. If startled they can turn and run - straight upwards, it seems - dislodging from time to time several loose, fist-sized stones that can easily hurtle like a shower of earthbound meteorites towards the heads of unwary walkers. Marmot burrows too, can be found on the higher slopes, wide, gaping tunnel-mouths driving deep into the hillside, and certainly as big as any fox's earth.

The Spanish frontier - looking due south

The last quarter to the Col itself is extremely steep, but the going on this section as a whole is reasonably easy. A marble plaque at the top marks your height: 2522m (8322ft). Below lies an unfolding vista, the seemingly endless range of the Spanish Pyrenees...and the first flavour of freedom for those men of sixty-odd years ago who were traversing these majestic peaks for a very different reason. But freedom, for the vast majority of French escapees at least, was to be cruelly short-lived. **(See 'Escape to A Spanish Jail', page 48)**

From the knife-edged crest of the col, take an easterly compass bearing of 80 degrees and follow a well-defined animal track along the side of a steep slope for approximately 300 metres, but take care while negotiating a short stretch of loose and crumbling shale. The sheer drop below won't do your future much good if you happen to slip.

Chemin de la Liberté plaque - Col de la Clauère

Lac de Clauère - an excellent place for a picnic!

As the animal track peters out, yellow and black "target-like" waymarks painted on rocks swing you to the right and sharply downwards through boulder-strewn gullies and across a series of snow-flattened grassy slopes.

Forty minutes later you'll arrive at the Lac de Clauère, a small and sparkling mountain lake tucked unexpectedly into a green shoulder of the upper slopes. The water is ice-cold, clear and inviting. If you're feeling brave, strip off and dive in. If you're feeling not-so-brave, a quick sock removal and sweaty feet submersion is thoroughly recommended.

NOTE: Until mid-July at least, there will be a lot of hard-packed snow on the descent from the Col de La Clauère to the Lac de Clauère. This in itself presents no great difficulty, but as all the yellow-and-black waymarks are painted on rocks (no trees at this height), many of them will be invisible until the last of the snow has melted. It's therefore recommended that you plan your trip sometime between the end of July and the end of September...before the dreaded snow buries those yellow-and-black blobs all over again!

Your height loss from the Spanish frontier to this point is 300 metres (990 feet), and the steep southwards descent is about to continue. From the lake, follow the yellow and black waymarks straight down towards a small waterfall which can be seen tumbling into the gorge of the Barranc de Clavera river which flows south to meet the Noguera Pallaresa river in the valley clearly seen below.

An hour later you'll reach the banks of the river itself. The clear, gushing mountain torrent is another welcome invitation to pause and get your breath back. Also to cool down if the sun is as hot and relentless as it usually is on these south-facing slopes of the Pyrenean range. Avoid unprotected exposure to high-altitude sunlight and remember to keep trowelling on your favourite brand of anti-burn cream!

Walking time from the Lac de Clauere to this point is approximately one hour. Keep following the yellow and black waymarks and you'll be led to another waterfall - higher and more impressive than the ones you've just passed - as you slither directly down to the water's edge. This time you cross the river and follow a path which leads you gradually up and away from the river (on your right) towards and then along the edge of a sweet-smelling plantation of spruce trees.

Just as you reach the treeline, the track widens out into a well-beaten path which then swings back sharply to the right and descends towards the valley below in a series of easy curves or lacets. If you've got this far without taking a wrong turn, then the rest is easy! There are no regular waymarks any more, but the well-beaten path meanders downwards until it meets another even wider well-beaten path which leads you (3 kilometres further on) to a "T-Junction" and a concrete bridge where the Barranc de Clavera torrent finally flows into and joins forces with the wider and more powerful Noguera Pallaresa River which flows west to east along the valley floor. During the 19th Century, in order to reach sawmills situated in the lower valleys, tough Catalan lumberjacks had to float and ride their felled trees down this mountain torrent in long convoys of rope-lashed rafts. It was hard and dangerous work and although the trade has long since died out, an excellent museum dedicated to the lives of these "raiers" can be found in the village of El Pont de Claverol, fifty kilometres south of Esterri d'Aneu. Walking time on the descent from the Spanish frontier to this point will be four hours. More if you stop at the suggested (and probably very necessary) "watering-holes"!

At the "T-Junction" and bridge close to the Noguera Pallaresa, you join the H.R.P path (Haute Randonnee Pyreneenne) which is clearly marked on the Carte de Randonnees IGN 1:50 000 map, Couserans Cap d'Aran-Pallars, Parc National d'Aigues Tortes (Pyrenees Carte No. 6). Turn right, and a few kilometres to the west is the ruined village of Montgarri, where French and Catalonian shepherds congregate at the beginning of July every year for a traditional blessing of their flocks. In recent years this blessing has become more of a public festival and tourist attraction as hundreds of hikers arrive from both sides of the border to claim their share of the wine, cheese and general jollity which is always on offer!

But instead of turning west to Mongtgarri, our successful Freedom Trail evader must turn left, east and then south towards safety and liberty in the town of Esterri d'Aneu! Your height now is 1500 metres (4950 feet), and there is still another 22 kilometres or nearly 14 miles to go before the final goal has been reached. Waymarks no longer exist, but the going is easy and it's impossible to go wrong as you follow the pot-holed track which hugs the banks of the crystal-clear river. If you're back-packing a tent, there are no limits or restrictions to the numbers of places where you can stop and pitch it. Cows and horses might sniff and stare, a passing forestry worker might rattle past in a battered four-by-four diesel truck, the odd mountain biker might bounce by, but apart from that you're all alone in a camper's paradise - no site fees, no wardens, no rules, no regulations. Except, of course, the usual self-imposed guidelines regarding litter, empty bottles, tins, flapping plastic bags and not setting fire to the surrounding forest. Enjoy!

One kilometre after joining the H.R.P. path, you'll pass a group of stone-built, slate-roofed barns on your left. High above on the hillside are the crumbling pillars of a disused lime kiln, close to which another way-marked walk heads back up towards the French frontier at Port d'Aula. The going is easy now, the slight, gentle descent barely noticeable as the track winds onwards along the valley floor. Another 4 kilometres and you'll pass a half-built and (at the time of writing) so far undeveloped ski de fond or cross-country skiing refuge.

The first real signs of civilisation are to be found in the village of Alos d'Isil, graced by a superb Roman bridge and 11th Century church. Here too, the pot-holed track ends and tarmac begins, so stride on for another 3 kilometres and the larger village of Isil hoves into sight. Here, in the shadow of yet another superb medieval church, the weary walker can

either stay the night or buy refreshments at the local bar-restaurant-hotel. A welcome stop indeed!

The village of Isil - Overnight stop recommended

History of the Freedom Trail
"Once is too Often!"

It's with those four words (and, one suspects, a wry sense of 'Geordie' humour), that Fred Greenwell from Tyne and Wear describes two major and dramatic events in his life - falling out of a burning Lancaster bomber over Germany in 1944, and scaling the Pyrenean peaks along his 'Chemin de la Liberté' three and a half months later.

***Flight-Sergeant
Fred Greenwell** in 1944*

At the age of twenty, Fred was a Flight-Sergeant Bomb-Aimer serving with 57 Lancaster Bomber Squadron R.A.F., based at East Kirkby in Lincolnshire. On the night of 24th February 1944, a large force of aircraft took off to attack an important ball-bearing production plant at Schweinfurt in central Germany. Fred Greenwell was a crew member of Lancaster DX-1 and flying on his thirteenth operational mission.

Several kilometres west of Strasbourg, in Alsace, the 'plane was badly hit and burst into flames. In the ensuing chaos, Fred and four of his comrades (including the pilot), bailed out safely. Navigator James Lightfoot and Air Gunner Frank Butler were killed. Within days, all the surviving airmen were prisoners of war except young Fred!

He had landed alone in a vast, snowbound forest of fir trees in the middle of the Vosges mountains. This region of Alsace-Lorraine had been returned to France after the 1914-18 war and promptly snatched back again when Hitler invaded in 1940, so officially Fred had bailed out over and was now standing on, German soil.

The full story of his four-month trek to freedom is certainly too involved to be included here, because as the days and weeks went by, his travels began to resemble more of an epic Homerian Odyssey than an airman's escape story. Fred's own personal and moving account of his adventures was recently translated into French by Alsace historian Andree Traxel. This 'Journal d'Evasion' is now a proud and welcome addition to the shelves of the Departmental Archives in the Historical Library of La Moselle.

"He was really very lucky," says Madame Traxel on the subject of Fred's escape! Helped, fed, clothed and hidden for days - often weeks - at a time by a succession of selfless freedom-loving individuals and French families, Fred at last found himself accepted by the underground movement as an official "parcel" to be passed southwards along the escape lines to the Spanish frontier.

On the 4th of May he celebrated his twenty-first birthday in Luneville, a small town south-east of Nancy in the departement of Meurthe-et-Moselle. Ten days later he was in a train travelling west to Paris accompanied by a young Belgian courier. From the French capital he travelled south to Toulouse, again by train and this time in the company of several silent and suitably disguised Americans who were also being "parcelled" down the line. It was during these two long and dangerous journeys that Fred realised the huge debt of gratitude owed by all escaping Allied airmen to the staff of French railways at every level and grade.

In the city of Toulouse - like John Franklin and Ray Hindle only two weeks before - Fred Greenwell found himself safely tucked under the all-enveloping wing of the legendary "Françoise" Dissard **(see page 36)**. "A humorous, good-natured, chain-smoking, indomitable woman with a huge adored cat," writes Fred. "The fingers of her left hand were much mis-shapen due to an encounter with a window frame in the course of a dramatic escape from the Gestapo. From the moment I came under the control of Françoise and her network I felt a lessening of tension and pressure. The breathing space of three golden days to rest and recuperate was more than welcome and it paid rich dividends when we came face to face with the Pyrenean peaks a few days later."

Accompanied by several Americans who had also been hiding in the Dissard safe house, Fred travelled south for the last time by train and

disembarked at a small mountain station which he thinks was Foix, forty
or so kilometres to the east of Saint-Girons. From Foix, another secret
escape route led south-west, skirted the town of Massat and climbed into
the mountains via the Col d'Agnes and the Etang (lake) du Garbet. Beyond
the Pic des Trois Comtes, the Spanish frontier was reached at the Col de
Montecourbas, roughly 16 kilometres (ten miles), north and slightly west of
the border with the Principality of Andorra.

This route was the one used by a well-known Ariège mountaineer and
passeur named Jean "Piston" Benazet. Time and again he led groups of
people to safety, at first (during 1941 and 1942), by the simple means of
driving them in his car along the valley road towards Andorra! Later, when
the Germans had occupied the whole of France and tightened their grip
on the border crossings, Jean took to using his secret chemin over the
mountains. By the Spring of 1943, he had made seven successful ascents
to the Spanish frontier with assorted groups of evaders. His eighth trip
on the 13th of June, however, ended in disaster. Climbing southwards
and upwards from the spa town of Aulus-les-Bains, Jean and his group
were ambushed by a German patrol. As rifle shots rang out, twelve men
were caught and arrested. The remaining six in the party (including Jean
Benazet), managed to escape under the cover of a sudden and violent
storm. Of the twelve evades arrested, nine were deported to German
concentration camps. Only four returned alive after the war.

In common with the vast majority of evading Allied airmen, Fred Greenwell
had very little idea of his exact location once the dangerous climb towards
the Spanish frontier got under way. Ascents were made in single file, each
one following blindly in the footsteps of the person in front: everyone
relying totally on the judgement and skill of the unseen passeur ahead.

Greenwell was the only R.A.F. man in his group. In addition to twelve
Americans there were several civilians, including a French teacher from
Paris on the run from the Gestapo, and a middle-aged Polish man with his
teenage daughter. Fred remembers his guide as a small, stocky man with
a large dog and an even larger umbrella. The route he was following was

in all possibility very close to the chemin used by Jean Benazet back in 1943; skirting the Etang du Garbet and climbing steeply towards the frontier near the Pic des Trois Comtes.

The first signs of trouble appeared during the hours of darkness on night one. The column had been halted by a steep-sided ravine and a foaming mountain stream which was spanned by a slippery assortment of felled tree trunks. The Polish civilian was carrying a heavy suitcase filled with his belongings and found it impossible to cross. In desperation he hurled his case into the void and, helped by the guide, eventually reached the far side. His daughter, however, was lying sobbing on the ground, too scared to move. No amount of pleading or encouragement would help to calm her fears and eventually the girl's father was forced to retrace his steps across the gorge in order to be with her. It was obvious then that their attempt at escape had failed. As heavy rain began to fall, Fred and the others stayed hidden near the banks of the ravine while their weary guide escorted the heartbroken Pole and his daughter back into the lower regions of enemy-occupied France. Nothing was ever heard of them again.

Many hours later, after the return of their ever-loyal passeur and an arduous climb through rain and cloud, Greenwell and his group finally reached a high mountain ridge which overlooked a steep-sided valley. Below, announced their guide quietly...lay Spain. The Americans (probably because they were Americans), promptly began a whooping and back-slapping display of uninhibited glee. A few even lit fires to dry their sodden clothes. In the midst of this hilarity, however, one voice preached caution. It was the voice of the teacher from Paris, Daniel Hericault, who knew only too well how friendly the government of General Franco's Fascist Spain had been with Hitler's Nazi Germany in recent years. Evaders caught near the frontier were invariably handed back to the Gestapo or the Vichy police, so the moral of Daniel's story was...having come this far, why get caught now without making a serious attempt to walk further away from the frontier and deeper into Spain in the hope of a less hostile reception?

In the event, they proved to be wise and worthwhile words. Their original passeur having returned to France, Hericault enlisted the help of a young Catalan guide from a hamlet in the valley below who led them towards yet another line of seemingly endless Pyrenean peaks. However after one more day and night - the night spent in an isolated farmhouse and barn with what Fred remembers as an unlimited supply of strong Spanish wine - the group finally reached the small town of Sort, 32 kilometres (20 miles), south of the Saint-Girons' Freedom Trail arrival point at Esterri d'Aneu.

Within days, the usual diplomatic interventions had taken place. Fred and his American friends were free men, soon to fly back to England via Lerida, Madrid and Gibraltar. Unfortunately, like all his French compatriots, teacher Daniel Hericault spent many months in a Spanish jail before being released to serve his country.

On the 24th of June 1944, Flight-Sergeant Fred Greenwell found himself on a train leaving King's Cross station in London, bound for Newcastle and the north. His four-month Odyssey was over. Fred was free to fight again.

Day Five

Isil (1200m, 3960ft)
to Esterri d'Aneu, Spain (948m, 3128ft)

Distance: 8 kilometres (5 miles).
Walking time: 2 hours.

*The 11th Century
Roman Church at Isil*

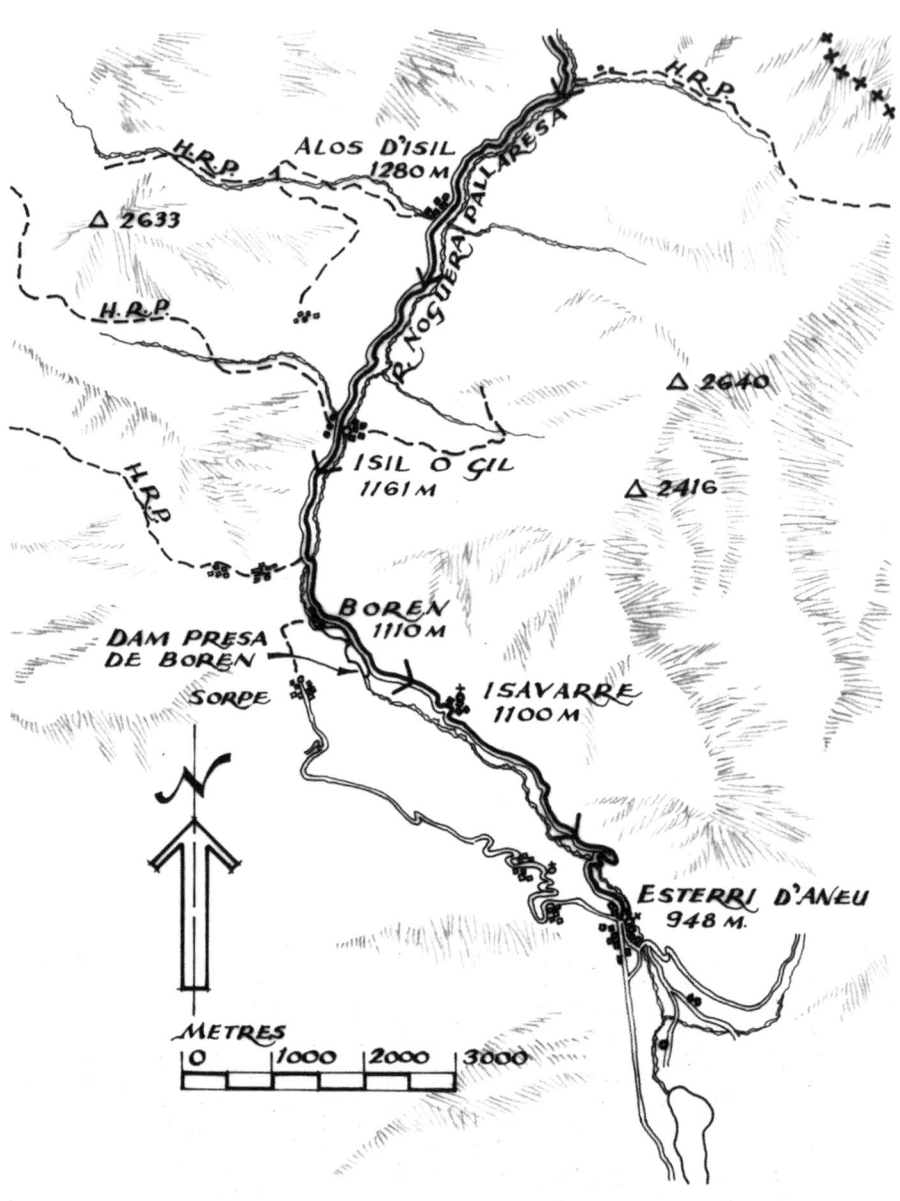

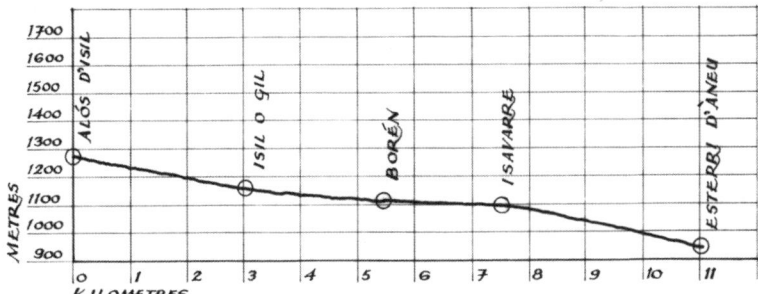

Only 8 more kilometres lie between you and the end of the Freedom Trail. On the way you'll pass the village of Boren which sits huddled at the northern end of a huge dam, the Presa de Boren, its deep dark green waters unusually still, silent and unruffled. Just down the road is the quaint and romantic-looking hamlet of Isavarre, and 4 kilometres beyond, after a series of hairpin bends, journey's end is to be found in the narrow streets of Esterri d'Aneu. It's a bustling little town with eight hotels (or to be more accurate, one hotel, one pension, four hostals and two fondas), several cafes, the usual range of shops and a tourist office. There is also a small, but very interesting museum situated in the heart of the old town. Two houses have been carefully preserved to illustrate exactly what life was like in a mountain village during the 19th century. Public transport is scarce but there is one daily 'bus service linking Barcelona, Lerida, Sort, Esterri d'Aneu, Vielha, and Les, near the French frontier. There is also a railway link between Lerida and Barcelona.

Esterri d'Aneu - end of the trail!

History of the Freedom Trail
"Ambush!"

It has been said before but is well worth saying again! During the wartime years, an escape down to and across the Spanish frontier - no matter how well-planned and expertly-led, could only succeed with a generous amount of help from that most fickle of all mistresses, Lady Luck.

Dutchman Samuel Timmers Verhoeven (better known by his nickname of Dick), certainly had more than his fair share of that commodity when the Good Lady decided to look his way on the morning of February 6th, 1944.

As fate (or luck!) would have it, that morning was Dick's twenty fifth birthday and he was part of a large group of escapees attempting to cross the frontier near the Col Portet d'Aspet, thirty seven kilometres west of Saint-Girons. It was a bright, sunny day and deep snow surrounded the barn in which the men were resting. Dick, suffering quite badly from the effects of an upset stomach, left the barn to obey an urgent "call of nature"! Moments later, as he crouched behind a tree only a hundred metres away, the morning calm was shattered by the sound of gunfire. Uniformed troops with Alsatian dogs were swarming up the hill to surround the barn.

It was perhaps the one thing feared more than any other by the men who were risking their lives for the cause of liberty. A classic and well-executed German ambush.

Dick Timmers Verhoeven was born in The Hague and brought up in Brussels, the son of a former Dutch Royal Navy officer who subsequently became a director of the Utrecht Life Insurance Company. At the time of the German invasion, Dick was finishing his studies at the Commercial High School in the Hague, and later worked as an insurance inspector in Brussels between 1941 and 1943.

It was early in 1943 that the Germans began to close universities in Holland and Belgium and decreed that all students be sent to forced labour camps in various parts of occupied Europe. Just as in France, thousands of young men made up their minds to either flee the country or go underground and join the resistance. In Holland the word "Engelandvaarder" was born, meaning literally "a voyager to England", from the Dutch words "varen" (sailing), and "vaarder" (a sailor). Very soon, that word "Engelandvaarder" was to became synonymous with freedom.

Many escaped over the North Sea, others to Sweden and Switzerland, even some via Finland and across Russia to India! The vast majority, however, escaped through France then over the Pyrenees to Spain, Portugal and Gibraltar. Many of these escapees were helped by the now well-established Dutch-Paris (or Van Tricht) Escape Line, and the Brussels-based Comete Line.

Provided with false German permits (courtesy of the Dutch-Paris Escape Line), Dick Timmers Verhoeven and three companions left Brussels for Paris on the night of 14th January, 1944. The four men travelled by train. "The false permits were very impressive," says Dick, "lots of stamps and German eagles!"

In Paris they waited for two and a half weeks while more forged travel documents were obtained and several more Dutch evades were brought together for the train journey south to Toulouse on the 3rd of February. There, in La Ville Rose, the party stayed overnight in a well-known and still existing restaurant "Chez Emile", in La Place Saint-Georges, whose rooms above the lively eating-place became a haven for many frightened foreigners and shot-down Allied airmen during the long and dangerous years of the German occupation.

Next day, the men took a train south to the small town of Cazeres, on the banks of the River Garonne. They spent the night in an empty house and met their two local passeurs, Mireille, and Pierre Treillet (codename 'Palau'). On the evening of the 5th of February, the group was driven in three gazogene or gas-burning vehicles, to an assembly point in the foothills north of the Forest of Arbas. There, a second convoy joined them, bringing the total of would-be escapees to thirty five. It was pitch dark, and as he crouched shivering in a ditch, Timmers Verhoeven tried first in Dutch and then in French, to communicate with the shapeless black bulk of the man next to him. When there was no reply, he spoke again in English, and discovered to his amazement that his new neighbour was an Australian air force pilot who had been shot down over Belgium two days before.

As the long night march to freedom began, the men were ordered to walk in single file and stay close to each other. But when heavy snow began to fall, many of them quickly became exhausted. Those fleeing from the occupied countries had suffered months and often years of hardship and privation and were certainly in no fit condition to tackle a major mountain chain at night and in the depths of winter.

Dick Timmers Verhoeven was ordered to bring up the rear and help one straggler who was suffering particularly badly. "I had to support the poor guy and force him to keep up with the others," he said. "Losing touch with the men in front meant getting completely lost and without a guide, map or compass in that bitterly-cold weather, it would have been fatal."

The snow stopped falling at dawn, but due to these sudden and severe weather conditions, the party was almost five hours late in arriving at its first stopping-off place, that remote barn mentioned earlier which overlooked a secondary road on the Col Portet d'Aspet west of Saint-Girons at a height of 1501 metres (4953 feet).

By then it was 11.30 a.m. and the sun was shining brightly from a clear blue sky. As he looked around at the men either talking quietly or lying slumped in varying degrees of exhaustion and fatigue in the confined space of the ancient sheep-hut, Timmers Verhoeven suddenly felt uneasy; that way up here, in broad daylight and on an open, exposed hillside, the group had got itself into a situation that was simply asking for trouble.

The Dutchman's hunch proved to be correct when only minutes after leaving the barn to relieve himself, a German patrol appeared out of nowhere. The ambush was swift, well co-ordinated and took the entire party completely by surprise. From his position behind a tree, Dick could see that the two passeurs, Mireille and Pierre, had also left the hut, followed by seven others.

As gunfire crackled across the open slope and dogs and soldiers closed in, Mireille shouted at these men to make a run for it back the way they had come earlier that morning. Timmers Verhoeven joined them, struggling uphill through deep, powdery snow, the pain in his belly now long forgotten in this new and desperate flight for life.

Below, the main group in the barn was surrounded and trapped. Realising that the fleeing survivors were leaving clear and easy tracks in the snow for the dogs to follow, Dick shouted at his companions to scatter. It was then that he and another Dutch friend, Gijs den Besten, came to a decision which in all probability saved their lives, although once again that fickle mistress Lady Luck was also there to lend a helping hand. What the two men decided was not to retrace their steps to the north and back into the forest of Arbas, but to swing west and south and fool the pursuing enemy by heading for the Spanish border on their own. "The frontier was only six miles away," said Dick, "and I had another, far more personal reason for not being caught by the Germans. Before leaving Brussels I had been given secret reports from the Belgian underground resistance, which were to be handed over to a certain Dutch Intelligence officer in Spain. I carried these micro-documents well folded in a toothpaste tube, half-filled to the top with toothpaste."

Using what cover they could, the two men ran down the hill in a south-westerly direction and hid in a ditch bordering the road. Two German soldiers came perilously close but passed on by.

Le Col Portet d'Aspet - The barn where Dick and his group were ambushed in Feb 1944. It is now a holiday home.

Later, the Dutchmen saw their arrested companions being driven off in two army trucks. The two passeurs Mereille and Pierre 'Palau' Treillet had also been captured, but later managed to break free and make a successful escape thanks, no doubt, to their intimate knowledge of the surrounding countryside. In all, twenty eight men out of the thirty five in the group were arrested and deported or sent to prisoner of war camps. To this day, Dick still doesn't know the full facts of what happened to those men, although he did find out long after the war (in 1990, to be exact), that the exhausted straggler he had helped during the night-time blizzard, another Dutchman called Hijmans, was deported to a German labour camp and subsequently died.

After lying low for an hour a bank of mist came rolling in, so the two men crossed the road and continued in their south-south-west direction, using a line of thick bushes as cover. They both knew that the frontier was close, but to reach it they had to cross the Pic de la Calabasse, whose snowbound peak soared up to a height of 2210 metres (7293 feet). This would have been a daunting enough climb for a fully-equipped climber in high summer, but for two unfit, untrained and badly-equipped young men from the flat polders of their native Holland, it was a challenge bordering on the impossible.

And impossible it proved to be. As darkness fell and the temperature plummeted far below zero, Gijs den Besten grew weaker and weaker. "His legs seemed to be frozen," said Dick. "Three times when we stopped for a moment of rest, he fell fast asleep. I had to slap his face to bring him back to reality. All he wanted to do was end it all."

Gijs den Besten was, in fact, slipping into that uncaring, dreamlike state which could only lead to death. By now, the men were trying to force their way onwards and upwards through a metre of powdery snow. At the end of a stretch which Dick Timmers Verhoeven found out later was marked on the map as the Plan du Rey, at approximately 1650 metres (5445 feet), he saw the lights of a village far down below on his left. Instinct said that he had to bear right if the frontier was to be reached but as the steep-sided valley in that direction was still plunged in the Stygian black shadow of a rising moon, Dick decided it was wiser and safer to turn left.

Again, that invaluable element of luck was with him, for although the route he had chosen actually led northwards again and away from the Spanish frontier, it was a move that undoubtedly saved den Besten's life. After a nightmarish descent, the two men eventually stumbled into the tiny village of Autreche, little more than a hamlet consisting of three groups of houses. In one house a light was shining, but as Dick started towards it, den Besten pulled him back, some instinctive sixth sense warning him of danger. Once again, Lady Luck had played her part well. The house with the light shining in it was a permanent German patrol station.

Helped initially by an old lady who fed them some thin onion soup, the two exhausted Dutchmen were then escorted by a ten year-old boy called Robert Peyrefitte and hidden in an empty house. "The poor lad was frightened to death," said Dick, "mainly because we kept falling asleep every fifty metres or so."

From then on, a family called Ribis took charge. Mother, father, married daughter and ten year-old son. Even today, nearly fifty five years after the event, Dick Timmers Verhoeven still marvels at the courage, fortitude and selfless devotion shown to him and his companion by those stout-hearted villagers of Autreche. The Ribis family not only fed and clothed them, but brought bandages and ointments in an attempt to cure Gijs den Besten's badly frostbitten legs.

When signs of gangrene appeared several days later in Gijs' left leg, Monsieur and Madame Ribis took an extraordinary and extremely dangerous decision to smuggle the young Dutchman out of their hamlet and into the nearest hospital more than thirty kilometres away in the town of Saint-Girons. There he was operated on in secret by a refugee Spanish doctor who had fled from the dictatorship of General Franco in 1936 and now found himself resisting another dictatorship in Nazi-occupied France!

The prompt surgery saved den Besten's leg, but he lost two toes, and during a long period of recovery was hidden and cared for by a variety of local inhabitants until he finally escaped to England eight months later.

Back in Autreche, meanwhile, after den Besten's departure, it had been decided that as soon as Timmers Verhoeven had regained his strength, he should make his way back to Toulouse in order to re-establish contact with members of the Dutch-Paris escape line. At the end of February 1944, the Ribis family organised a grand farewell party. "Boiled ox-head in a huge pot with herbs and potatoes," remembers Dick. "The whole family was there to wish me luck, and a lot of their friends as well. Fantastic! After many whispered au revoirs at about midnight, a local farmer led me through the bushes to the neighbouring village of Saint-Lary, where I was hidden in a trailer hooked on to a 'bus. I was disguised as a local Frenchman, Basque-type beret included!"

Next day during the journey to Saint-Girons, the 'bus was stopped at a German zone interdite or forbidden zone checkpoint. Everybody out, careful scrutiny of identity cards, permits, luggage, even a thorough search under the seats. Fortunately, the fully-loaded trailer of market produce and animals being towed behind the 'bus was not inspected, but from his hiding-place and through the wooden side slats of the vehicle, Timmers Verhoeven had an extremely uncomfortable close-up view of a bulky German officer holding a straining Alsatian dog on a short leash. The dog started to bark loudly, its attention obviously drawn to the strong human scent emanating from the Dutchman concealed inside. "I was not smelling at my best that morning," recalls Dick with a certain irony!

But as the German moved forward to investigate, Lady Luck waved her magic wand yet again. Less than a metre from Dick's hidey-hole was a wicker basket containing three frightened cats. As the dog snarled and bayed at the side of the trailer, they broke into a series of high-pitched and plaintive miaows. Much to the Dutchman's relief, the guard jerked at his dog's leash, uttered a loud and surly "zuruck!", ("get back!") and ordered the animal to keep its mouth shut.

In the busy Saint-Girons market place, many local people converged to help with the task of unloading the trailer. Bit by bit they slid back the thick tarpaulin top, and in the general hubbub, Dick eased himself out to mingle with the crowd and become just another paysan who was helping with the morning chores "I carried barrels and God knows what," he said, "and at one point I saw a German officer with a red lining in his open greatcoat who seemed to be staring at me with a curiously fixed expression. Fortunately nothing was said, so I presumed his thoughts were far away, dreaming perhaps of his "bloody heimat!" (homeland).

Still unnoticed and unsuspected, the Dutchman boarded another 'bus that was to take him to the railway station of Boussens, 30 kilometres to the north. As Dick left, Madame Ribis was there once again, that selfless and courageous lady wishing her jeune evadé yet another last and fervent "bonne chance et bon courage!"

By that evening, Timmers Verhoeven was back in the city of Toulouse. With a certain amount of difficulty he found his way once again to the 'safe house' of Chez Emile, the restaurant in La Place Saint-Georges. There, to his amazement and delight, he found two of his fellow Dutchmen who had been ambushed with him at the barn on the Col Portet d'Aspet. They too, had escaped and found their way back to La Ville Rose. In all, there were now more than twenty fugitives of various nationalities hiding behind the closed shutters on the upper floors of Emile's restaurant. For the others, this was their first experience of travelling south to face the snowbound peaks of the Pyrenees, but for Dick Timmers Verhoeven and his two friends, the nightmare was about to begin all over again. A second journey south and a second attempt to cross the forbidding mountain chain that separated them from that now all too-distant dream of freedom.

Early in March 1944, Dick and his two friends from the first debacle at the Col Portet d'Aspet, plus eight other newly-arrived Dutch escapees, were all moved to a safe house in Blagnac, on the outskirts of Toulouse. There they waited for nearly three weeks while new forged documents were obtained for the men and they were visited by two important members of the Dutch-Paris Escape Line. To Dick's surprise, he was severely criticised by the organisers for having disobeyed orders from the passeurs and heading for the border instead of turning back into the so-called safety of the Arbas forest. Dick defended his decision by revealing that he was carrying secret documents from the Belgian resistance movement and was promptly asked to carry several more secret documents, also destined for the Dutch Intelligence authorities in Spain!

On the 25th of March 1944, the men were moved south into the departement of the Haute-Garonne and assembled for their escape attempt north of a town called Bagneres de Luchon. As well as a series of guides, this time armed with Sten guns, the party comprised fifteen Americans, twelve Dutchmen, three Frenchmen, one Canadian and one exhausted Belgian pilot who had been a prisoner of war for three and a half years before managing to escape and make his way south.

The Canadian, a Mustang (P51) fighter pilot called John Hartley Watlington, had been shot down over northern France in June 1943 and had been "on the run" ever since. He had fought with the Maquis, lived for a few carefree weeks in a chateau owned by a former Governor-General of one of the French colonies, and had even attempted to escape back to Britain in a fishing boat. This attempt failed when the boat sank and most of the party was captured.

One of Watlington's most prized possessions was a beautifully tailored overcoat which had belonged to the French Minister of Agriculture, Monsieur Henri Queuille, who had earlier escaped to Algiers. The coat had passed through several hands before being handed down to the Canadian, who looked upon it as an extremely valuable asset which would help him to face the freezing temperatures and deep snow of the Pyrenean peaks.

The crossing took three days and involved the scaling of several peaks over 2000 metres. "The last lap was terrible," said Dick Timmers Verhoeven, "and especially hard for the worn-out Belgian pilot." As for Watlington, he was chewing endless benzidrene tablets in order to keep going. These tablets formed part of his pilot's escape kit and he'd kept them intact all through his long months on the run. They came in a small envelope on which was printed a warning that one should be taken only under extreme conditions of fatigue and only every six hours. "But," said Watlington, "I was cheating badly, being so pooped out with this vertical stroll that I was eating the damn things as you would candy! And I don't remember feeling any less exhausted for it, either!"

But at last, at 6.30 in the morning of Tuesday, March 28th, the men stood almost disbelievingly on the frontier with Spain. After what they had been through, the descent was pure joy. John Watlington tucked the tails of his precious overcoat between his legs, used a branch as a rudder, his feet as a brake, and quite literally slid the rest of the way to freedom on his backside. His one pang of regret was that as he stumbled to his feet at the bottom, he noticed that the speed and friction of that joyful descent had ripped the tail of his coat to pieces. It would never quite be the same again!

Later that year, Dick Timmers Verhoeven reached England and enlisted as an officer in the Royal Artillery. After active service in Java he was demobilised in 1947.

In October 1996, the Dutchman returned to the cabin which still stands on the Col Portet d'Aspet west of Saint-Girons. There, at a commemoration ceremony attended by his former passeur, Pierre 'Palau' Treillet, and the son and daughter of the courageous Monsieur and Madame Ribis, Dick Timmers Verhoeven unveiled a memorial stone which pays everlasting tribute to the guides, helpers and evadés de guerre of all nationalities who sought and fought for liberty between the war-torn years of 1939 and 1945.

Dick Timmers Verhoeven and his wartime passeur Pierre 'Palau' Treillet - Oct 1996.

Epilogue

Samuel 'Dick' Timmers Verhoeven died in July 2003. In June 2004 his three sons and two daughters retraced and hiked their father's escape route across the Pyrenees. In the words of Elizabeth Harrison, former secretary of the Royal Air Forces Escaping society...

"not all memorials are made of bronze or stone"

Keith Janes ...hiker, historian and webmaster at www.escapelines.com

Le Chemin de la Liberté
Suggested Equipment List

Please note that it is very important to keep the weight DOWN. Go for as light a load as possible, certainly **no more than 12 kilos (26lbs)**

- ☐ Walking boots
- ☐ Walking socks (2 pairs)
- ☐ Walking gaiters
- ☐ Breeches/Shorts/Trousers
- ☐ Sun hat
- ☐ Rucksack + waterproof rucksack cover
- ☐ Sleeping bag
- ☐ Karrimat
- ☐ Gortex survival bag or lightweight tent
- ☐ Knife, fork, spoon
- ☐ Mug
- ☐ Plate/Dish
- ☐ Cooking utensil
- ☐ Small first aid kit
- ☐ Two water bottles or camel "suck" bag
- ☐ Waterproof anorak and trousers. *(guides advise AGAINST ponchos, too dangerous in mountains)*
- ☐ Tin opener
- ☐ Small torch *(head-torches even better)*
- ☐ Sweater
- ☐ Gloves + Woolly hat *(very important at altitude if below freezing)*
- ☐ Spare clothing
- ☐ Washing/shaving kit
- ☐ Towel
- ☐ String and penknife
- ☐ Sun tan lotion

- ☐ Insect repellent *(horse-flies can be bad on Spanish side)*
- ☐ Foot powder
- ☐ Passport/Camera/spare films
- ☐ Walking stick(s) or Leki pole(s)
- ☐ Brew kit/rations... *eat what you like to eat!*
- ☐ Matches *(preferably waterproof)*
- ☐ Tissues/Toilet paper
- ☐ A sense of humour
- ☐ Bin liner for inside rucksack
- ☐ Small poly bags for rubbish *(no dustbins in mountains, all litter, empty tins, etc, must be carried back to base)*

Survival Food

Brew kit

Sardines

Dried fruit/nuts

Fruit (apples, oranges)

Stew

Any personal choice!

Water

Chocolate, energy bars

"Boil in the bag" dehydrated food

Notes

Notes

Notes

Notes

_____

_____

_____

_____

_____

_____

_____

_____

_____

_____

_____

_____

_____

_____

_____

_____

_____

_____

_____

_____

_____

Notes